The
Mindsets Factor
in
Ethnic Conflict

The Mindsets Factor in Ethnic Conflict

A Cross-Cultural Agenda

Glen Fisher

INTERCULTURAL PRESS, INC.

Intercultural Press, Inc.
P.O. Box 700
Yarmouth, ME 04096 USA
207-846-5168

Book design and production by Patty J. Topel
Cover design by Patty J. Topel

Printed in the United States of America

02   01   00   99   98   1   2   3   4   5

Library of Congress Cataloging-in-Publication Data

Fisher, Glen, 1922-
    The mindsets factor in ethnic conflict: a cross-cultural agenda/Glen Fisher.
    ISBN 1-877864-60-9
        p.   cm.
    1. International relations and culture.   2. Ethnic relations—Political aspects.   I. Title.
JZ1251.F568   1998
305.8—dc21   98-5153
                              CIP

Table of Contents

Preface

Analyzing ethnic conflicts, either formally or informally, has become a prime concern for a wide range of people involved in post-Cold War international affairs. More effort is going into trying to understand their causes, their politics, and their implications for the way that the international community is organized to manage them. The international relations process itself has come to revolve more around policies regarding ethnic conflicts, peacekeeping activities, humanitarian assistance, conflict resolution, and, frequently, coordinating the roles of the many nongovernmental organizations (NGOs) that become involved. Sometimes the occasion to analyze is both urgent and dramatic.

Understanding ethnic conflict has many facets; the perspectives of many specialties, disciplines, and administrative fields are indispensable. However, and this is a prime consideration for the approach pursued here, ethnic conflict also includes an especially significant psychocultural dimension which has to receive substantial emphasis on the analytical agenda. Too often this facet receives only passing and superficial attention.

This study, then, is concerned with the role that *mindsets* play in ethnic conflicts and the importance of the cross-cultural task often posed in understanding them. Why "mindsets"? And what advantage is to be gained by focusing on set ways of thinking to better understand the ethnicity dimension that is now so salient a consideration in managing world affairs?

To begin with, it is unavoidable. Addressing ethnic conflict is, after all, an exercise in coping with mismatched worldviews and patterns of perception. It is in collective mindsets that one finds explanations for each ethnic group's way of defining its issues and problems, for its image of the larger society and other groups, or for any special mode of reasoning by which information is processed. Even ethnic identity itself is a kind of mindset, and an inquiry into mindsets is an effective way to take cultural uniqueness, in its deeper psychological meaning, into account.

It is also practical. Since mindsets imply rather fixed patterns of beliefs and implicit assumptions that are not easily subject q change by threat or persuasion or amenable to compromise, they constitute the hard reality that has to be addressed and dealt with in conflict situations. And attention to mindsets helps one be conflict-specific in analysis. How one views the way that the city of Jerusalem should be governed, for example, is a function of very different mindsets that are brought to bear from distinctly Israeli and Palestinian perspectives. Their fixed ways of thinking do not provide an easy basis for the "rational" discussion and compromise that is urged on them by outside mediators. Understanding a stand-off in mindsets is to the point.

Our current need to diagnose a wide range of ethnic conflicts and prescribe remedies in the course of managing international affairs is, not surprisingly, the stimulation for pursuing the discussion developed in these pages. But with a comprehensive literature already available on ethnicity, nationalism, and ethnic relations, some consideration has to stand out as still being insufficiently addressed to merit an additional venture into this huge field. Most obvious is the fact that much of the conflict management being carried out in the international community today is being undertaken by outsiders, that is, by people who are foreign in one degree or another to the conflict area. They have to surmount a cultural barrier of their own to probe critical psychological forces driving conflict and do it *while the conflict is in progress.* Or, in the interest of preventive diplomacy, do it in anticipation of conflict. Their analyses, projections, and judgments have to home in on moving targets—for which much of the existing literature serves mainly as background orientation.

The concern here is for *practitioners who must manage conflict situations on the spot,* and this is written with these "outsiders" in mind. While many generalized resources regarding the nature of ethnicity or nationalism are available, the practical problem is one of diagnosing the conflict-specific behavior with which one is confronted and of judging the prognosis for resolving it—or at least containing it. To a large extent, the task for mediators, peacekeepers, relief agency personnel, negotiators, policymakers, and even journalists is to analyze the conflict as seen by the groups involved, to understand critical perceptions in some detail, and to estimate the degree of feeling, antagonism, or intransigence that must be taken into account, which, in most cases, implies a task in cross-cultural analysis because it is an *ethnic* conflict.

What is expected from this study needs to be made clear at the outset. It is not a comprehensive review of ethnic conflict theory or literature; it does not quarrel with the many insightful aids to analysis provided from all the disciplinary vantage points from which the subject is addressed. The purpose is simply to add perspective that seems undertreated and to direct more methodical attention to a range of underlying psychocultural factors driving ethnic conflict which too often is left to the self-assured operating assumption that, after all, human nature and human reactions are obvious enough. I have tried to do somewhat the same thing for addressing other aspects of cross-cultural interaction in my book *Mindsets: The Role of Culture and Perception in International Relations*.[1] The effort here is to extend that direction of inquiry more specifically to ethnic conflict. In fact, the subtitle of this book could well have been "the role of culture and perception in ethnic conflict."

As in any problem-oriented analytical process, the objective is to see causes that produce effects in the real terms of a given time and place—a Sarajevo under siege, or a Northern Ireland on the verge of negotiating an end to a long-standing dispute. How is one to explain, in an accurate and dependable way, the logic of the confrontation? How does one pose the right questions to oneself or to the area specialist in order to zero in on the critical elements in each case that explain confrontation and determine its path?

Knowing that a conflict is a thousand years old, or that political power has been abused by a majority, that atrocities have been committed, or that there is competition for economic advantage may well be germane. But even in descriptive detail, such background facts provide a rather abstract basis for judging just what action is to be taken. Two cases of ethnic confrontation may present themselves in similar contexts, but evolve in very different ways, producing, perhaps, no more than strikes and demonstrations in one instance, but brutality and civil war in another. Sometimes one will have to understand

---

[1] Glen Fisher, *Mindsets: The Role of Culture and Perception in International Relations*, 2d ed. (Yarmouth, ME: Intercultural Press, 1997).

rather precisely just how two ethnic groups can live in harmony for a generation and then suddenly erupt in intransigent warfare.

In organizing the material that follows, it is assumed that most readers will be concerned with analyzing ethnic conflicts because they are actually involved in an ethnic conflict environment, trying to formulate strategy for managing ethnic conflict, or perhaps the reader is an analyst or a student working on a case study research project. Having such a specific case problem in mind will enhance the use of this text, since the intellectual agenda developed here can be applied as one goes along. Brief illustrations drawn from a wide range of conflict scenarios will be used to clarify points made, but no single sample case study will be presented. In general, references will be confined to those needed to credit sources directly used or suggest an efficient way to explore a subject in greater depth.

It should also be noted that the focus here is on the kinds of ethnic conflicts that have particular significance for international practitioners, rather than those that come up in the course of managing pluralism in established democratic societies. This is a choice made for delimiting a very large subject, although it is a rather artificial one, as much of what is said here will also apply to conflicts at home which, while less internationally prominent, also have a cross-cultural dimension. Managing diversity in a pluralistic society is, after all, a matter of recognizing that some culturally defined patterned differences in thinking and outlook exist. While the stress placed on analyzing the psychology of racial prejudice and group discrimination is obviously essential, it might be useful to also frame the problem in terms of ethnic conflict and pursue the ways in which it is cultural conditioning, or at least subcultural conditioning, that produces social distance between groups. In this approach, much more attention would go into analyzing the cultural substance that has to be bridged in achieving cross-cultural understanding and harmonious relations.

The need to augment our resources for analyzing ethnic conflict has been made clear to me as well as to many others by participation in several agenda-setting activities at the United States Institute of Peace. Having long pursued a special interest in the psychological and cross-cultural dimensions of other aspects of the international relations process, I found that ethnic conflict seemed to invite my attention. At the Monterey Institute of International Studies, teaching several graduate seminars which were focused on analyzing ethnic conflict has also served to help organize my thinking on the subject. A brief period spent at the United States Institute of Peace as a Guest Scholar provided the occasion and the facility to explore some applied aspects of the subject. My own perspective here starts with my graduate training in sociology and cultural anthropology, followed by pursuing a career as a Foreign Service Officer generally assigned to places where cultural differences within countries mattered—the Philippines, for example. When on an assignment as Dean of Area Studies at the State Department's Foreign Service Institute, I also found that problems related to ethnicity frequently had to receive strategic attention and that it was a subject that had to be included in many area and country courses conducted for officers prior to their assuming posts abroad.

The question that has concerned me, therefore, is how differing mindsets lead people to perceive and reason in unique ways in the course of international interaction and, especially, how culture explains patterned differences in mindsets. Sometimes the effects are to be noticed in direct person-to-person communication. At the other end of the scale, mindsets help explain thinking at the institutional level as people establish policies and, in turn, respond to them. International negotiation is a clear case of culture and perception at work. Ethnic conflict is an even clearer case.

In attempting to provide conceptual tools for helping practitioners work with this cross-cultural dimension, I have found that the term "mindsets" has worked well. It highlights psychological processes that are germane to a given analysis while avoiding more academically mysterious jargon; and, in a way, its popular meaning suggests an intellectual agenda. In essence, the proposal here is to extend that direction of inquiry to its relevance for diagnosing field problems in ethnic conflict.

Diagnosing Ethnic Conflict: Taking Culture and Perception into Account

Ethnic conflict of one sort or another has been around for a long time, and few would try to understand the international relations process without giving it full consideration. But it can be argued that what is now new, at the turn of the century, is that ethnic conflict has assumed more central and critical importance in the task of managing an ever more interrelated international system. While such conflicts have lost relevance as testing grounds for ideological competition in Cold War strategy, they have gained importance for their political and economic impact on the stability of the international community. Ethnic conflict has evolved into an aspect of international relations with new facets. It therefore places certain new demands on our analytical capabilities if problems in post-Cold War world affairs are to be adequately understood and addressed.

The cases prompting attention are varied, indeed.

For example, the republics of the former Soviet Union with their unique ethnic compositions have become new actors on the international stage. Ethnic identities that had been suppressed in accordance with the communist conception of society and government have resurfaced with spirit and determination as the Soviet Union has dissolved into an uneasy set of national entities which allow renewed recognition of ethnic divisions. Groups such as Tajiks, Uzbeks, and Kazakhs assume international significance, and events in that area now become a function of these identities. The dissolution of Yugoslavia and the out-of-control human dislocation that went with it have posed major strategic problems for the United Nations, NATO, and all the foreign offices that have needed to react. In Africa, ethnicity dominates: ethnic groups that have never been fully melded into their rather artificially defined nation-states continue, in their lack of societal cohesion, to produce near chaos for the peoples of that area. Even long-established nations such as France and Germany are confronting problems in digesting immigrant ethnic groups into their national societies, as is the United States despite its origins as a supposed ethnic melting pot. Current international migration often involves peoples whose motivation is not necessarily to be "melted" into a new sense of who they are.

The discussion to follow argues that analyzing ethnic conflict is a demanding endeavor in its own right. As contrasted with the government-to-government disputes usually treated in the international relations field, ethnic conflicts often are confrontations that reflect interests deriving from a common bond of culture that are being expressed without formal governing authority. It therefore requires an approach that will use conceptual tools that may differ from or, at least, be added to those that are routinely used for describing and analyzing other more frequently pursued aspects of relationships among nations. The key in the definition is "ethnic," which implies injection of exclusive cultural orientations and group identities into the diagnosis—cultural characteristics and a group experience that most likely will be alien in some degree to those who have to manage things from a perspective outside the conflict itself.

The recent historical record shows that we are not always very adept at this, especially as new non-Western societies have proliferated as players on the international stage. We note that people responsible for international decision making often operate from a traditional Western vantage point and, in the process, fail to recognize their own intellectual ethnocentricity and their dependence on conventional conceptions about the ways that nations behave, or should behave. When confronting societies and cultures (e.g., ethnic groups) that follow less familiar patterns of logic, political leaders, military strategists, even diplomats tend to project their Western experience and analytical orientation without sufficient effort to take contrasting cultural realities into account.

Within the international relations discipline itself, where time for analysis is more abundant and assumptions are more likely to be examined in the interest of academic objectivity, the record is not much more encouraging. Much of the scholarly production, along with the prescriptions of pundits and journalists, fits into a Western mold of thinking. When area specialists and practitioners with long exposure to given foreign areas *do* provide a reliable picture of differing social reality, what they have to say seems "unreasonable" and is, therefore, dismissed or second-guessed. It clashes with established habits of thinking and reasoning.[1]

---

[1] For decision maker's problems in accepting and using the specialist's input, see Alexander George, *Presidential Decision-making in Foreign Policy: The Effective Use of Information and Advice* (Boulder, CO: Westview Press, 1980).

One of the most dramatic examples of the havoc that can be wreaked by inappropriately projecting conventional assumptions is the case of Vietnam as recalled by Robert S. McNamara in his *In Retrospect: The Tragedy and Lessons of Vietnam*. Going back over his experience as Secretary of Defense at the time, he cites disaster after disaster in decision making as the right questions about local cultures were not asked and events were ethnocentrically interpreted, especially as attempts were made to quantify as many factors as possible to make the conflict fit into a systems analysis framework. Consequently, a war was pursued in a very foreign place with little appreciation for the real motivation and purpose that drove the Vietnamese in both the North and the South—and consequently little appreciation of the inappropriateness of the objectives and strategy pursued by the United States. This was the more ironic as the decision makers at the center were known as "the best and the brightest" in the American system. But it was a brilliance that did not travel well across contrasting cultural systems.[2]

There is a similar tendency to be superficial in addressing ethnic conflict today where, by definition, a cultural gap is to be taken into account. The implicit assumptions that go with Western thinking are projected, often out-of-awareness, because they are habitual; analysis too easily retrogresses to the patronizing conclusion that the people involved are irrational, are too emotionally affected for clear problem solving, perhaps are too inclined to follow leaders who are opportunistic or even unbalanced, and, in any case, are prone to ignore their own best interests.

The task for many practitioners then is to attain an in-depth understanding of *somebody else's ethnicity* and

---

[2] Robert S. McNamara, *In Retrospect: The Tragedy and Lessons of Vietnam* (New York: Times Books, 1995).

the view of the world that goes with it and to understand what, specifically, it has to do with the problem at hand. While an outsider's distance and detachment may actually enhance objectivity, a substantial cross-cultural obstacle course is presented. It is especially apparent to those who have to work "close up" to conflicts in carrying out policies or who have to improvise on a daily basis in execution.

This last point deserves emphasis here, for managing ethnic conflicts or attending to the physical and social damage they create has placed ever larger numbers of cultural outsiders into ethnic conflict situations, leaving them to make their own judgments regarding immediate and local issues. A lot of ingenuity is required. Often there will be few precedents or standard operating procedures to be relied upon—how to get a shipment of relief goods from a port to a refugee camp where it is needed, how to encourage local officials to maintain even-handed law and order, how to maneuver around roadblocks, how to build a team of local assistants into an effective unit when they are selected across ethnic lines or are expected to work across them. A lot of ethnicity-related judgments have to be made on the spot.

A routine example to illustrate the problem at the micro level: Early in my time in the Philippines after the opening of an American Consulate in Cebu City, I had undertaken a familiarization trip around the island of Mindanao, part of our new consular district. This included traveling a sixty-mile stretch of then very marginal road through the heart of the Philippine Muslim area, from Cotabato to Lake Lanao. This was an area in which Phil ippine authority was accepted very tenuously at best by the Moros. The previously arranged plan was to pick up a Philippine Constabulary escort as precaution against problems with the road and especially with law and order. When we arrived at the Constabulary camp, all appeared ready.

But the officer in charge of the escort, a Moro himself, wanted a private word with me. He explained: He had his orders; his men and vehicles were ready, and there was no question as to his willingness to go. But he wanted me to make the final decision. My Filipino assistant and I would be safer without the escort than with it. The escort would *invite* attack; an unarmed American (Americans were then popular with the Moros) would be better off alone. So it was on-the-spot decision time, and it involved judgments regarding motivations and perceptions in the local conflict, Moro ethics as far as strangers were concerned, attitudes toward Philippine authority, and how deeply local people felt about it all. The escort was left behind. The condition of the road did, in fact, pose a need for assistance, but local people were warm, friendly, and helpful. The plan to use a military escort that seemed so logical from a distance did not mesh with the outlooks and attitudes that would determine how things would work out in the real event.

This need to take culture-specific patterns of thinking into account has already been recognized in many phases of international life—in person-to-person interaction of many kinds, in negotiation, in managing businesses abroad, and in extending development assistance. Here we simply add the activities of the mediators, peacekeepers and enforcers, emergency assistance teams, journalists, policy decision makers, and concerned citizens who face the difficulties inherent in trying to make sense of conflicts driven to a significant degree by ethnic differences. It is easy, of course, to empathize with fellow human beings. Clashing interests, and the fact of conflict and violence itself, evoke human emotions and reactions that have a certain universal quality. But adding "ethnic" makes empathy more elusive. The generic quality of human motivations has to be calibrated for the press of culture on a case-by-case basis, often in dramatic degree, and this modification can be critical to accurate understanding.

I will argue in this book that to capture a sense of how people whom we designate as members of ethnic groups are programmed to perceive themselves, perceive other groups, identify with the interests of some larger society, define issues, and channel their feelings and emotions is a matter of understanding *collective mindsets* which, at the risk of repetition, are basically alien to the outsider.

Applying Psychological Explanations of Conflict

In analyzing any conflict, the objective is to determine what the problem is all about from the perspective of the antagonists themselves; in effect, to determine where the parties to the dispute are "coming from" psychologically. In analyzing international conflict, using psychological insight and conceptual tools has a long and productive track record. Much of the field of political psychology is devoted to it. The role of perception and misperception, and especially of enemy and threat perception and the uses of propaganda, are well researched. Psychological warfare is a subject unto itself. Studies of aggression, the authoritarian personality, stereotyping, and the nature of prejudice are familiar. Cognitive mapping and operational codes as well as psychological profiles and psychobiographies are often-used approaches to understand leaders in psychological terms. Images are analyzed and attitudes are surveyed. Decision-making analysis uses terms like "groupthink."[3] And there are studies

---

[3] For a review of these approaches, see Yaacov Y. I. Vertzberger, *The World in Their Minds: Information Processing, Cognition, and Perception in Foreign Policy Decisionmaking* (Stanford, CA: Stanford University Press, 1990).

of deep emotion that apply to international processes covering such matters as hate; grieving; and reactions to fear, violence, deprivation, and even fatigue. Nationalism itself is a subject of psychological analysis.[4]

However, and this is the point of departure for most of the discussion that follows, these applications of psychological analysis tend to be aimed at understanding ways in which human beings are generally and universally alike in their psychological behavior. People grieve for past personal and collective losses, hold prejudices, misperceive, hate, and so forth, as general aspects of being human. This is highly relevant, of course. But in looking for psychological explanations for *ethnic* conflict, we are also interested in the ways that psychological processes and reactions *differ* or are modified precisely because of the way that culture and ethnic experience have bent and molded the more universal proclivities that we expect to be in force.

Since each ethnic conflict is a confrontation of particular ways of seeing things that go with being socialized in and sharing the experiences of the ethnic groups in question, each case of ethnic conflict is different from any other. This is what the mediator, conflict manager, or relief administrator has to work with in each instance. Abstract and theoretical formulas for understanding ethnic conflict in general may help, but they will not be enough. In working directly with conflict, specific patterns of perception need to be identified and understood. And for all the research that has been done on mediation, negotiation, and conflict resolution, there is seldom sufficient emphasis on the critical relevance of ethnic-specific psychology itself.

Perhaps a digression here would be useful to make it

---

4   As one sample, see Donald L. Horowitz, *Ethnic Groups in Conflict* (Berkeley, CA: University of California Press, 1985).

clearer how our emphasis on mindsets fits into all the other academic or disciplinary approaches that are used to address ethnic conflict, especially where practitioners are concerned. There is often a difference in objective between the scholar and the practitioner. In part, this is a matter of the level of abstraction at which understanding is sought. The scholar tends to be oriented toward theories and principles, and one sees much of this in scholarly production. The practitioner has to face a concrete problem. An analogy from the field of politics might make the point regarding abstraction. At one level, one might be interested in comparing political systems or comparing political philosophies as a way of understanding political behavior as such—requiring a high level of abstraction. At a somewhat less abstract level, one might be interested in how political parties as institutions operate in a political system in a given country and in the varying ways they choose their strategies for gaining political positions. At a more concrete level, one might be interested in just what makes people vote the way they do in a specific election, in how they perceive specific leaders and issues, and in what buttons are pushed to make people respond. And finally, the question might be brought down to what makes a single given leader or individual perform in an idiosyncratic way.

All these levels have their place. For our present purposes, a more midlevel kind of abstraction seems most useful, somewhere at the next-to-last level described above. Thus we will focus on the need to understand the patterns of thinking characteristic of specific ethnic groups. Note the importance of the word "patterns," which implies prevailing statistical modes that are usual and normal, but not necessarily subject to 100 percent conformity—we are not looking at idiosyncratic behavior, important though this might be in actual analysis. The multidisciplinary approach used here will draw broadly from the fields of sociology, applied anthropology, and social psychology.

It might be noted further that differences in level of approach also affect the kind of data and information sought. When the level of abstraction is high and the purpose is scholarly, analysis is best done deliberately, after the fact, with data and information carefully tested. This is time-consuming, measured research. For policy making, and most especially in field operations, analysis is made *before* the fact or during the event with the best information available at the time. Again, the analytical or intellectual agenda being proposed here is aimed essentially at the practitioner who must achieve optimum understanding and make the best judgments while the action is in progress.[5]

Thus, turning to the idea implied in what is popularly called "mindsets" seems appropriate to the applied nature of the problem and to the effort to understand the perception habits in play in each ethnic conflict situation. Mindsets is a commonly used term. Webster defines it as "a fixed mental attitude formed by experience, education, prejudice, etc." It cuts through much of the technical vocabulary and terminology that go with the social science disciplines which deal with psychology or culture and fits in with other words we commonly use such as attitude, stereotype, image, thought pattern, or worldview. We often try to understand people by trying to figure out "where they are coming from." And it is, after all, mindsets that have to be understood if one is to anticipate the patterns of thinking and reasoning that are so central to conflict management.

---

[5] This contrast of objective is well stated in David Newsom, "Foreign Policy and Academia," *Foreign Policy*, no. 101 (Winter, 95-96): 52-67. It is discussed in greater depth in Alexander George, *Bridging the Gap: Theory and Practice in Foreign Policy* (Washington, DC: United States Institute of Peace Press, 1993).

For example, the conflict in Northern Ireland might be seen superficially as another in the category of stand-offs between religious groups. But the mindset approach would probe more deeply and note how reactions reflect a larger internalized complex of outlooks that involve relative social position, economic advantage or disadvantage, political disputes, degree of identification with English traditions, differing memories of the past, and much more, in addition to the surface religious alignment.

We might provide an agenda of things to come in succeeding sections by quickly previewing some of the main ethnic-specific, mindset-related problems that many practitioners, in the role of being their own consultants, will have to cope with in ethnic conflict environments. It will, of course, be impossible to probe psychological programming to its last detail. But it is possible to propose priorities for what typically needs to be understood. The chapters that follow are thus arranged as "problem areas." I suggest five.

A Five-Point Analytical Agenda

1. *What are the key ingredients that go into these "fixed mental attitudes" that come into conflict?* This is the question of just what people as members of an ethnic group know and believe. What substance goes into ethnic mindsets? What is contained in the information and belief base, whether real or imagined, that will be brought to bear in interpreting events and issues? It is to be noted that this line of inquiry is a different quest from simply describing the conflict itself and the objective facts surrounding it. In determining outlooks, "facts" as they appear in mindsets might or might not be true. The test is whether they are *believed* or are held as implicit assumptions. Even the historic details of group relations, which the out-

side historian might establish with reasonably scientific accuracy, are of relatively little importance in determining behavior as compared with the way that history is remembered in ethnic group lore. The empathy needed in field operations, then, depends on an exploration of what makes up the collective psychological or cognitive world of the group that one is trying to understand. And this has to be taken seriously. That which is taken for granted in Armenian, Rwandan, Tutsi, or Sri Lankan Tamil outlooks is not simply a matter to be corrected by reasoned persuasion in negotiation, but a matter of well-implanted basic data to be taken into account at every stage in diagnosing ethnic conflicts.

2. *In terms of a given conflict, who is to be included as part of an ethnic group?* Typically there is a practical question as to just who can be expected to respond to ethnic appeals or line up to be counted in political activities. This is a function of both group and individual self-images and images of other groups and the larger society itself. While the facts of language, kinship, and local social structure would seem to determine membership—and, indeed, the exclusion imposed by other groups or by the larger society may leave little choice—effective identity as a member of a specific ethnic group is, in the final analysis, a mindset.

A further and very fundamental problem for a conflict manager often consists in fine-tuning an analysis of ethnic loyalties. For example, there is the question of just how strong, fixed, and single-minded a sense of identity will be or what other identities might be appealed to in the interest of resolving conflicts. The fact that groups may live together in harmony for many years, even intermarry, only to erupt in rigid ethnic confrontation as their societal circumstances change demonstrates the way that a sense of identity can be relative. In the modern world people often carry multiple ethnic or national identities in their heads. One might, at the same time, be Basque, Spanish, and European. In some circumstances the narrowest identity might not pose a problem, but in others, it might emerge as intractable. Often the problem for the conflict manager is in anticipating which identity will be the controlling one.

3. *How rigidly "set" are the mindsets that are pertinent to a conflict?* Judging the depth, inflexibility, and emotional charge of basic beliefs and assumptions is a critical dimension of the inquiry, since these factors would strongly influence the *degree of intransigence* to be found in the conflict. This often has to be estimated as strategies are chosen and decisions are made concerning what is to be done if conflict is to be resolved or at least contained. When will negotiating and reasoning be adequate? When will stronger action be needed?

It has to be recognized that at the more extreme end of the intransigence range, there may be instances in which careful estimation will indicate that a conflict simply is not subject to resolution at a given stage or amenable to the kinds of revised perceptions, mind changing, or tension reduction that would be required for successful mediation or negotiation. Then the judgment might have to be made that humanitarian concerns or the well-being of the larger international community will require containment by outside force, at least for a period of time. This is fundamental in United Nations decision making, of course—when to send in a peacekeeping contingent.

In many conflict situations mindsets are less set or emotionally charged. In such cases, one might expect solutions to be achieved simply by providing occasion and means whereby the parties themselves can enter into dialogue and, in effect, work out their own problems. That is, their opposing complexes of beliefs and attitudes would be psychologically subject to de-escalation and compromise, or other patterns of thinking are available to decrease rigidity in positions taken. Or perhaps a little more psychological support is needed. Intervention by a third party might help bridge mild intransigence. Or providing a place to shift the onus for compromise might serve a psychological purpose. But again, choosing the strategy involves a psychological estimate.

The point is that conflict is not only a function of *what* concerns, perceptions, beliefs, and emotions are in contention, but the *depth* at which they are fixed in the mindsets of the groups involved. It is not only a matter of cataloguing mindsets content, but of estimating the "set" part.

4. *Do the solutions that are proposed for conflict resolution themselves raise cross-cultural considerations?* Mindsets come into play in the way that people perceive and react to solutions for conflict as they are proposed and, subsequently, as they are put in place. Justice, for example, is to be found in the eye of the beholder, as are the need for retribution, prescriptions regarding the ideal government role, or a conception of the ideal society. The reasonable solution carried in the minds of outside mediators whose perspectives revolve around a need for international order and stability and the well-being of the international community might seem much less reasonable in the narrower social perspective of a partisan group in Bosnia, for example, where so-called "ethnic cleansing" has had—in the eyes of these beholders—an obvious appeal.

5. *What outlooks pertain to the role that the international community or its representatives is expected to play*? Managing ethnic conflict will depend heavily on the way that those involved relate psychologically to the larger world community and mold their expectations regarding international activities undertaken to address their problems. While we assume that the way that ethnic groups perceive their status within national states will be important, how they perceive their interrelationships within a region or in the international community also needs to be taken into account. This will have much to do with any sense of legitimacy accorded to outside conflict management in the first place and with the kind of intervention that is easily accepted.

When Is a Conflict an Ethnic Conflict?

What we mean by "ethnic" is often not clear. We have problems with definitions. Diagnosis is then complicated by the question of deciding just when a given conflict is, in fact, "ethnic," with the idea that the confrontation is driven at least in part by outlooks and perceptions that have roots in a significant cultural uniqueness to which a group holds loyalty—and which are at odds with those of some other group or mainstream collectivity. But the exact role of ethnicity may be uncertain, as in many cases loyalties and identities overlap. The key task is anticipating just when people will relate to an issue on the basis of being members of their specific ethnic group, when as citizens of their country of residence (if national boundaries and ethnicity do not coincide), or when, perhaps, as members of some larger transnational ethnic identity that extends beyond national boundaries, such as Jews or Kurds.

The problem is made no easier as our vocabulary for dealing with group loyalties is somewhat convoluted. What is a "nation"? Do the Kurds or Jews mentioned above, for example, constitute a nation wherever they are? When is ethnicity simply a matter of pluralism within a nation? In practical application, when is a person a Greek Cypriot rather than a Cypriot Greek? When does a sense of being one ethnic group coincide with a nation-state that has delimited territorial boundaries, exercises control, and deals as a discrete entity with other nation-states in the international system? We speak of nationalism or ethnonationalism when ethnic groups turn chauvinistic, and of nationalistic movements when people unified by ethnic identity seek political independence.[6]

For convenience in the discussion here, "nation" will be used to mean a nation-state as consistent with general usage in international relations—a governing entity. In this usage, ethnicity and nationality might, or might not, coincide. Or, in what we have come to designate as civic societies, the shared national experience might itself produce a kind of overriding ethnicity. The closeness of a given citizen's identity with a nation and with that nation's culture, government, and national purpose can vary greatly—which is at the root of our problem in definitions, of course.

---

6 Walker Connor, for example, addresses ethnonationalism in his book *Ethnonationalism: The Quest for Understanding* (Princeton: Princeton University Press, 1994). See also Anthony Smith, *National Identity* (Reno, NV: University of Nevada Press, 1993). For a larger research project categorizing groups as minorities with differing types of political dynamics at work, see Ted Robert Gurr, *Minorities at Risk: A Global View of Ethnopolitical Conflicts* (Washington, DC: United States Institute of Peace Press, 1993).

The Distinctive Aspects of Ethnic Conflict

More precisely, then, how does designating a problem as ethnic affect our analytical approach?

Possibly the first consideration for people in the international relations business is that the units of analysis usually change. As noted above, rather than calculating the positions and actions taken by sovereign states with governments that make policies and send representatives to staff embassies and to vote in international organizations, the focus shifts to the behavior of communities that act and react as culturally defined units which might or might not have separate governing authority. Thus, rather than analyzing the intentions of South Africa or Canada, it becomes a matter of making sense out of—depending on the issue—the motivations of Zulus or Quebecois. Not a new problem, but a new shift in emphasis.

More important, the assumed logic for collective behavior shifts from that expected when political forces seek advantage within a civic and contractual conception of government to motivations and outlooks based on the ethos of the group designated as ethnic. The idea of ethos is important. In seeking the rationale behind behavior based on ethnic identity, one looks for an underlying mosaic of belief, religion, sentiment, collective memory and mythology, special outlooks inherent in language, and so forth which go with the ethnic group's common culture. To get at this, conceptual tools may have to shift somewhat from those ordinarily used in political science and comparative political fields to include those used by area and comparative culture specialists, sociologists, and anthropologists.[7]

---

[7] For an emphasis on culture, see Kevin Avruch, Peter W. Black, and Joseph A. Scimecca, eds., *Conflict Resolution: Cross-Cultural Perspectives* (New York: Greenwood Press, 1991).

Further, as ethos implies a focus on the psychological dimension of culture, analytical attention needs to turn to those systems of worldviews, implicit assumptions, and ways of thinking that are learned out-of-awareness in the course of being socialized into an ethnic group. For the outsider, this is a considerable challenge. It becomes something of a search for a personality inventory at the level of group psychological norms and patterns, or a probing of ethnic character. The substance for ethnic analysis thus becomes much more profound than a simple appreciation for folk dances, traditional foods and costumes, or the customs that can be easily observed that so often go with popular conceptions of ethnicity.

The basic fact of life for most practitioners dealing with ethnic conflict versus other kinds is that they are more obviously working from their perspective *outside* the cultural conflict, not that of those on the inside. Therefore, whether they are mediators in a negotiating room or peacekeepers patrolling a street, they are less likely, without effort, to see things as their clients do. They will not feel the emotions or empathize naturally with the sense of rightness and morality that, for the protagonists involved, makes positions taken and actions carried out in conflict seem so normal. As noted above, when we say that a conflict is ethnic in nature, we are saying that a cultural divide exists between the antagonists themselves and, in all probability, between the outsider's ethos and those of all sides of the conflict as well. In sum, ethnic conflict is a study in cross-cultural psychology. While this is generally understood to be a background factor in most international relations problems, it is explicitly the problem in cases of ethnic conflict.

This leads to an important reality too often overlooked: ethnic conflict can be seen as a *normal consequence of cultural differences*. It is not pathological behavior per se, although it is dysfunctional from the point of view of civic government where modern democratic processes call for compromise and identification with the well-being of the larger society. The analyst, then, must start out by not looking so much for what went wrong in group relations, but by trying to understand how conflict has been a product of each group doing what comes as the norm to it by virtue of the cultural process. Each culture, of course, instills a belief that its ways of thinking are, without question, the correct ones. Culture engenders a deep sense that what one customarily does is human, moral, and sanctioned, while that which others do from a differing cultural prescription is abnormal, possibly inhuman, immoral, and an outrage to decency. This is an essential aspect of the function of culture; it is a basis for conformity that makes social life and group survival possible in the first place. People have to be enculturated into the patterns of thinking of their societies for social systems to work.

The reader will see that the above statement might be too strong for practical application in many cases. It needs modification. This ethnocentric impulse varies in strength from culture to culture and from person to person. There is also the reality that cultures are not entirely different from each other, that they overlap and change, and that they often provide ways of dealing with foreigners who do not share the same socialization process. At times individual behavior can stray from the group pattern, and in modern pluralistic societies, civic cultures place a value on broad acceptance of differing norms. But it is useful to start from the premise that ethnic conflict has a built-in source, especially when differences are deep and involve critically important patterns of belief and thinking.

Emphasizing Perception's Role

Thus, ethnic conflict rises from situations where there probably will be no agreement as to what is intrinsically rational and reasonable. Perception and reasoning do not conform to uniform standards. This tends to frustrate people in the international relations fraternity, especially those who prefer to conceptualize the international relations process in terms of analytical models in which nation-states act rationally within their circumstances to gain their objective interests and in accordance with recognized power relationships and economic forces as befits the world of political alliances and trade agreements. It goes against the grain for those who tend to minimize the importance of values and ethics as serious factors in world affairs. This school of so-called realism traditionally has downplayed cultural differences. Again, we recall the lessons of Vietnam, among many others, where the critical variables were not those that lent themselves so readily to the systems analysis approach that was in vogue in decision making at the time, but rather everything that went into actual Vietnamese perceptions of the conflict.

In ethnic conflict those supposedly universalistic, rational, and reasonable sets of assumptions that often underlie strategic calculations do not go far. For instance, one cannot "deter" ethnic conflicts by military threats or by diplomatic negotiation, as might be the case in more established nation-to-nation affairs. Local culture does matter. In fact, values, a sense of morality, sentiments, and emotions do explain what is going on, and these are not universal but unique to each ethnic group in their special detail and in their combination in cultural systems. If we can think of intellectual approaches as ranging from rational and realistic at one end of the spectrum to culturally specific at the other, ethnic conflicts have to be approached more from the culturally specific end.

The argument being pursued here, of course, is that whatever competence one has established in more traditional analytical approaches to working in the international arena, and however applicable these may in fact be in addressing ethnic conflict problems, much is to be gained in addition by more purposely focusing attention on the most central factor of all: *the case-particular way that people, as members of an ethnic group, are programmed to perceive the issues.*

Perceptions in play constitute a kind of hard data that have to be considered as forthrightly as conditions affecting logistics or resources for maintaining law and order. They often carry a heavy load in explaining the positions taken and the behavior we observe that may seem extreme by world community norms. We recall the genocide in Rwanda, the mindless destruction of Sarajevo, or the intransigence in insisting on the nonnegotiability of settlements on the West Bank. We have had to deal with suicide bombing carried out by Islamic fundamentalists, among other acts we judge extreme.

Explaining perceptions then, and especially ethnic-specific perceptions, is a large part of the art of diagnosing ethnic conflict. They are subject to many factors, as we know: the emotions of conflict itself—fear, deprivation, reaction to violence and death, and the often dramatic significance of the issues at stake. But when there is a group pattern in the perception and reasoning process in the conflicts that we designate as ethnic, that is what has to be taken into account if analysis is to be useful and methods for addressing conflicts are to be effective.

Since practitioners have to become their own diagnosticians, an ability to pose ethnic conflict problems in terms of the way that culture molds perception processes seems vital. If nothing else, it helps practitioners recognize when they are inappropriately projecting their own culturally generated implicit assumptions onto problems of ethnic origin or are simply operating on the conventional wisdom that goes with established diplomacy and ways of managing other types of intergovernmental matters. To be sure, taking culture and perception into account is not an entirely new challenge to the expected competence of international professionals. But given the increase in cases of ethnic conflict that have to be addressed, rechecking the diagnostic approach seems worthwhile.

We now proceed to examine in more detail the five ethnic conflict problem areas which seem especially to invite mindsets analysis. And with that, we will explain further some of the conceptual approaches that go with this psychocultural emphasis.

1

First Problem Area: Understanding a Conflict from an Ethnic Group's Point of View

The rather obvious first objective in trying to understand the dynamics of an ethnic conflict is to figure out precisely what ethnic culture has to do with it. Yet this part of the inquiry is often pursued only superficially. Practitioners too quickly become absorbed in the conflict management process itself, concentrating on techniques for negotiation and tension reduction or, necessarily, on the sheer complications of orchestrating positions in decision making and the logistical problems of doing anything at all. By way of conflict analysis, it is all too easy to focus mainly on historical development, current descriptions of what is going on, the issues, and the political context, but otherwise treat one conflict much like another. The emphasis tends to be on what is going on, rather than *why*. Or, in the rush to do something, the "why" is pursued superficially, rather as an afterthought.

The point is that conflicts have an internal logic, that people are sane, that from their point of view positions taken and actions pursued seem reasonable, or at least the best choice in the perceived circumstances. *The question then is just what is it about a given ethnic culture that makes up a point of view*? How do circumstances and events come to be perceived? What basic beliefs and implicit assumptions plus what added bits of selected and filtered information make up the substance that is fed into the reasoning process? Because this input will be specific to the social and cultural milieu in which each conflict is generated, it is this "logic" that has to be captured. It needs to be understood even though it may not seem so "logical" by the time all these psychological explanatory causes have led to a full-blown conflict. Making policy choices, after all, depends on making predictions as to what steps will lead to what results within the *actual reasoning processes that are at work in the field situation.* Therefore, we emphasize the importance of area analysis as psychocultural analysis to advance this objective.

Our contribution to this analytical effort is the argument that mindsets themselves have explanations and that the "reality" that exists in them is not necessarily the same as that established by the facts or the historical review of events that might be provided by journalists, country handbooks, or the reports that result from fact-finding commissions such as those dispatched by United Nations agencies in preparation for conflict intervention. Being able to describe mindset substance in some detail is as important as describing the action on the ground.

In effect, the question starts with what—for the groups in question—are mindsets made of? What is the database that has been supplied by culture in the form of group-learned, group-shared, and group-transmitted bits of information and knowledge? And what has been added, as newer information has been processed to mesh with the old ? That which comes in via mass media with all their potential to both inform and distort, or from propaganda, or through actual experiencing of events meets what is already there, that is, earlier learning, folklore, traditional education, and so forth, which set the stage for the way that subsequent data is absorbed. It all mixes together to supply the grist for the mill to produce the outlooks and ways of reasoning that have to be dealt with.

In the rush to get things done in conflict areas, important factors explaining mindsets are often overlooked or disregarded because, even if sought out, they seem peripheral or exotic. For example, ways of resolving conflicts over cattle theft in Somalia or other parts of East Africa would seem to be a low-priority concern until it is recognized that the local councils that traditionally attend to such matters are expected to play a significant role in resolving conflicts in general. It is part of the culture and has an important impact on larger as well as more mundane conflicts. In understanding Palestinian refugees' refusal to be absorbed in places like Jordan and Lebanon over the years, a rather close look is required at all the collective ways of thinking by which being absorbed comes to mean giving up the claim that Israelis violated their land rights when they were forced to become refugees in the first place. And appreciating the force and persistence of these beliefs requires still deeper probing of beliefs about land, family, and identity as well as collective memories of contesting these rights over centuries. Why, to Serbian leaders, is the battle of Kosovo that took place in 1389 still taken so seriously, and why in ethnic conflicts do Serbian Orthodox priests, in unexpected role behavior, come to join their local militants as combatants?

Or, to go back to my modest problem in traveling through Moro territory in Mindanao, why could I expect more friendliness to me as an American visitor than would be accorded to Filipinos from other parts of the Islands? Specific mindset factors could be taken into account, including remembered experience of warm relations through earlier American administration and guerrilla collaboration in World War II, but also a surviving pride and sense of honor in legends of very credible resistance offered by the Moros when the Americans first took over the area. It is boasted that the .45 revolver was invented specifically for them; smaller arms in use at the time did not stop Moros. Whether true or not, I still do not know, but the belief was part of local lore, local culture. In short, these seemingly obscure particulars can make an important difference.

Much detail goes into the cognitive composites that we call mindsets. Just what do parents teach their children? In schools, what is the mix between the transmitted outlooks of one's ethnic group and such subjects as science and mathematics that everyone in a modern school learns? Exactly what are the tenets of religion, the themes of song and folklore, the nature of the heroes, the worldviews of popular novelists and philosophers? What does one learn in the process of making a living? What does one learn to desire, or to fear?

It is in untangling the resulting predispositions to perceive things in an ethnic-specific way that area and intercultural specialists have most to contribute. These specialists should be able to establish what fundamental data from area studies and cross-cultural analysis mean in psychological terms, that is, as customs of the mind—or culture's programming, to use a computer analogy. In this way, area studies background supplies an insight into, and even an achievable empathy with, an ethnic group's way of thinking.

Part of our effort to see how culture provides a psychologically logical explanation for conflicts requires a somewhat closer look at the process by which mindsets become functions of ethnicity. With this in view, a quick review in this chapter of certain basic concepts regarding culture and patterns of thinking may be in order. (A more extended discussion of the way that culture programs thought and perception can be found in my earlier book on mindsets.)[1]

A Closer Look at the Ethos Concept

In working situations, one does not normally go around checking out peoples' mindsets. It is all too easy to simply dismiss strange perceptions and ways of reasoning as incompetence, the product of deviant personalities or, in overseas situations, as the result of obscure "political" factors. However, perception and reasoning behavior is not usually that capricious. It will probably make sense if one can capture the specifics in the matrix of knowledge, assumptions, beliefs, values, and concerns that people will rather automatically draw upon to supply context and meaning to issues in question. But this is not easy when one is working cross-culturally and the conflict is, by definition, a culturally loaded problem. The analytical objective, then, is to probe the master programming that goes with ethnicity to predispose the outlooks that have come into confrontation. Or, in ethnic terms, to capture the ethos, at least as far as basic outlooks are concerned.

In this regard, the theory of the relationship between culture and modes of personality is germane and can be briefly summarized here. That theory starts with the idea that in the ordinary course of trying to cope, people necessarily have to *project* meaning onto events and, even more so, onto abstract issues and problems—a basic tenet of perception psychology. Something has to be added

---

[1] Fisher, *Mindsets.*

from cumulative experience and memory to provide that sense of meaning. This is basic to human functioning. It would be exceedingly demanding if people had to look on each new event and address each new problem with completely fresh eyes, as though learning counted for nothing. Life would be chaotic. Rather, people do learn and come to organize their minds so that they have in reserve a system of meanings to project onto the world and onto its events and their own role in them. Language itself is a learned organizing device in that it helps name, categorize, and interrelate the items of one's existence. Knowledge is remembered; experience adds up, to be used again and again. It all gets cognitively organized into models for thinking and reasoning which can be applied as occasion demands, somewhat like computer software—very effective, very efficient. Thus one perceives and reasons by formulas (mindsets) that are not easily overridden.

This function of organized mindsets is easily illustrated. After all, even the sight of a gun would be of little significance if in the perceiving process one did not have a formula for thinking about guns, what they can do, the circumstances in which they are used, and the possible intentions of those who might have them under their control at the moment. The gun itself broadcasts no special meaning; some kind of programming of the mind has to be drawn upon.

But it is also essential in culture and personality theory to note that social life depends on people being programmed in somewhat the *same way* in order to be able to project the *same meaning* or "common sense" onto all matters that involve group interaction, communication, and cooperation. Enter culture in its psychological dimension. Everyone has to sing from the same songbook if there is to be harmony in group relations. This, of course, is the function of being socialized in the culture of one's group and internalizing its patterns of thinking and reasoning;

culture supplies the songbook. A potential for *ethnic* conflict is posed when two groups are singing, that is, perceiving and reasoning, from somewhat different scores. A collection of people stands out as an ethnic group precisely because it does hold a unique set of psychological perspectives that are socially learned, practiced, and transmitted from generation to generation. If I were Armenian, for example, I would be well programmed not only to share outlooks that pertain to the daily routine, but also to recall as other Armenians would recall what the Turks did to Armenians long before I was born.

I noted earlier that in looking for ways to make the existence of ethnicity-related mindsets understandable, "ethos" is a useful concept. Accordingly, social scientists have studied the relationship between culture and personality. A wide range of formulations and applications has been pursued. The term "national character" is frequently used, although there have been problems with it for some scientific purposes. Studying what is going on as people try to communicate across cultural boundaries is an exercise in culture and personality analysis, since differing subjective meanings reflecting differing patterns of personality are injected into the process of coding and decoding messages.

Applying the culture concept in this way is becoming more familiar as people talk increasingly about corporate or organizational cultures, meaning, in effect, the ethos of such entities. Inquiries are also being made into the probability that values and ways of thinking supplied by culture have a lot to do with economic performance.[2] A work ethic, for example, is a personality trait

---

[2] In relation to economic development, see Lawrence E. Harrison, *Who Prospers? How Cultural Values Shape Economic and Political Success* (New York: Basic Books, 1992). For a discussion related to mindset factors in modern large economies, see Hedrick Smith, *Rethinking America* (New York: Random House, 1995).

molded by culture, and even small differences in this regard can be very significant in the way that societies are organized to engage in agriculture or produce goods in factories. We talk about "civic culture" as group psychological predispositions required for the participatory give-and-take that goes with democratic processes. Cultural orientations often come up in setting the strategy for international merchandising and advertising: how are tastes, feelings about prestige, or desires for given products affected by a particular culture's programming?

The term "personality," like "culture," suffers from the many meanings it has, but in this usage, it implies a summing up of all the knowledge, beliefs, implicit assumptions, acquired likes and dislikes, philosophical outlooks, values, sentiments, fears and anxieties, and styles of thinking on which mindsets are based—and suggests that one's culture is the source for much of one's personality. Therefore, groups with a common culture will present a pretested and sanctioned pattern of personality as the preferred choice for its members.

Thus, we come to the key point for our purposes in diagnosing ethnic conflict: If ethnic groups are so designated because they hold some degree of uniqueness in culture, then it is useful to recognize that they also reflect a similar degree of uniqueness in the character and personality of group members. That is, an ethnic group comprises a community of shared patterns of beliefs, sentiments, and all the rest indicated above (though complete uniformity would not be expected). *Analysis, then, requires a focus on just what these acquired mental customs are and how they program perceptions of the issues around which conflict revolves.*

While human beings are fundamentally alike everywhere, it does not follow that they think alike. In most cases, ethnic conflict is generated because two communities with differing psychological programming, outlook, and identity are bumping against each other as they live intermixed in a given geographical area, or as minorities existing within a larger national entity. In the latter case, they may well share an even more encompassing larger national culture. But in categorizing a group as "ethnic," we imply a significant variation in culture, or subculture. What sets the group apart is a degree of self-recognition of common roots, shared history, a special collective experience, often a common place of origin, and their own customs, values, and sentiments that provide the basis for thinking that "we" are unlike "them." If this social distance is further solidified by such central mainstays of culture as language, religious institutions, literature, economic activity, and an in-group social structure, the psychological basis for ethnic identity and belonging is strengthened.

Hence, we are concerned with the implications that in-group culture in its psychological particulars holds for conflict behavior. In simpler times before people traveled so much or were so plugged into international communication and media networks, delineating the boundaries of ethnic groups was easier. One ethnic group could more easily ignore another. And in some corners of the world, isolation and cultural homogeneity are still pervading facts of life. In the problem areas that demand our attention today, the borderlines of ethnicity usually are less clear-cut, both in terms of subdivisions of larger populations and in the psyches of individuals.

Still, when the ethnic button is pushed—perhaps by circumstances or by a leader or propaganda—culturally packaged mindsets are triggered. This means that there will be distinct limits to resolving the conflict through intellectual persuasion, by establishing the "facts," or prescribing an outsider's notion of justice. In accord with culture and personality theory, these patterns of thinking are not easily changed; and from the point of view of the social group, they serve an essential function. They constitute, as a matter of course, the "what-I-learned-in-kindergarten" preparation to get along with the group and survive in the physical and social environment for which the group's culture is an adaptation. Much of culture is learned informally and practiced without conscious choice, having passed from one generation to the next for a very long time.

Further, cultures work best when the elements fit together as interrelated parts of a system, when customary ways of thinking support each other, when a pattern of reasoning that works for one realm of activity will not be too different from that used in another realm. Therefore, changes are not easily introduced, for the system resists them in straining toward consistency—as does the human mind. Cultures have tenacious continuity, and they demand conformity. End result: individuals also hold mindsets that seek consistency and resist yielding too easily to compromise and persuasion.

A Stage Is Set for Conflict When Cultures Collide

It should be apparent that interaction would not be automatically harmonious in cases where people who have undergone their basic socialization in one culture meet people who have undergone theirs in a different one. Pose an issue or a problem, and conflict becomes a probable consequence of any cultural differences in ways of believing, perceiving, and reasoning that are the norm for the cultures in question. Consider, as an example, the case of opening up the American West. One issue was land ownership and use. In the thinking prescribed by American Indian cultures, people generally did not actually own land in the sense of individuals claiming it, paying for it, or fencing it in for individual exploitation.

Early treaties with them that seemed to legitimize occupation of Indian territories did not mean the same on the two sides—hence real ethnic conflict, violence, the Indian reservation system, and a series of tragedies with effects that persist to the present. Or in France, a regulation regarding appropriate dress for girls attending the public schools which prohibited the Muslim headdress unleashed ethnic conflict with the resident Algerian population where feelings about covering girls' heads ran deeply.

While unadulterated socialization in a single cultural system is not necessarily the case in most instances of ethnic conflict today, when people do identify as members of an ethnic group and put on the glasses that correspond with that identity, they will be looking through a cultural lens which preprograms conflict to the extent that people are led to perceive issues differently.

Again, it is perhaps misleading if we go so far as to say that conflict is the natural product of ethnicity, but it is useful to recognize that when culture serves its vital function in providing a design for group life, it also sets the stage for conflict as cultures program their adherents to think in differing ways. However, one should expect culture's programming to persist; after all, resisting rapid change is a socially useful quality, since culture provides a pretested pattern of customary behavior that works for people as they come and go as members of the group. We often see evidence of this persistence, of course. When ideologically inspired attempts in social engineering are made to urge people to forget their ethnic ways in the interest of the well-being of the larger society or nation, the force of ethnic cultures tends to prevail. Years of pressing the communist ideology onto diverse cultures in the Soviet sphere of control did not erase embedded ethnicity. And in the Philippines, years of American attempts to implant democratic precepts of civic society did not

33

readily produce what the United States hoped would stand out as the "showcase of democracy in the Far East."

In the context of managing ethnic conflict, two follow-on considerations regarding culture's programming seem especially pertinent. One is that the very persistence of the patterns of thinking described above helps explain the endurance of ethnic confrontations over generations. In fact, the conflicts themselves become part of the cultural database, and the sense of conflict is passed from one generation to the next. So patterns for dealing with a running conflict become customary, normal, a traditional way of thinking. Enemies become traditional enemies; hatreds and resentments are taught and learned, often without considering alternatives. In the case of areas with a long history of severe ethnic conflict, it is not surprising that prescriptions for dealing with an enemy are amply provided for.

In the Balkans, for example, Paul Mojzes suggests that because of a "heritage of horror," revenge and spite have become cultural norms. He notes that atrocities and calculated savagery are chronicled in a mixture of history and folklore that goes back to at least the eleventh century. Defeated soldiers were blinded; impalement was practiced. Villages were pillaged and burned out of spite. Women, children, even relatives of the tyrants involved were subjected to the most violent cruelty. Mass murder was very much a part of the picture. Through the Balkan wars, the perpetrators included the range of ethnic groups in the area: Turks, Greeks, Bulgarians, Serbs, Macedonians, Albanians, and Montenegrins. During World War II, these inherited norms of violence were continued by Serbs, Croats, Muslims, and the Communist-led *partizans*. And while modern instances are censured as violations of human rights, throughout most of this history, the violators gained hero status within their own circles, both in legend and in political office.

So this theme becomes part of the cultures of the area, a component of mindsets that persists today. Children learn such norms as a matter of course.[3] Much the same would be found in most conflict-prone areas.

The second consideration involves the way that culture leads its clients to feel the inevitable correctness of their own cultural ways and, therefore, the *incorrectness* of alien cultural patterns and the people who practice them. Because people learn their culture largely out-of-awareness and in the confines of their own group, its ways feel "right" to them, unquestionably natural and human, moral, and emotionally comfortable. If a member of one's own group fails to stay in line, that "abnormal" person is punished and may become an outcast and identified as evil. Such deviance seems not only an affront to common sense, but to all the values that underlie feelings of community and belonging. (A liberal sense of "live and let live" is, from an anthropological point of view, an acquired taste, but one that is quite possible in more complex cultural systems.)

Therefore, when one ethnic group meets another, the "normal" ethnocentric predisposition would be to view the other as a mass of deviants, outside the limits of trust, subject to correction, punishment, certainly ostracism—something less than human and less deserving of the ethical restraints that one would honor within one's own group. How ethical prescriptions might be limited to one's own group is illustrated by the judgment in the Koran that while it is a sin to kill a fellow believer, beyond that, religious doctrine is less precise. How about allies such as U.S. Air Force personnel killed in a terrorist bombing attack in Riyadh in 1996? Islamic scholarly opinion ruled that in that case the bombing as political

---

3 Paul Mojzes, *Yugoslavian Inferno: Ethnoreligious Warfare in the Balkans* (New York: Continuum, 1995).

protest was also a sin, but it was subject to some discussion.

It should be noted that many cultures do contain customs for getting along with out-groups. Practices regarding hospitality are well known in the desert Middle East. In the modern world, cultural exchange programs have become institutionalized as positive practices in many places. But the nature of culture itself and the processes by which personalities are molded in the course of being enculturated into the patterns of the group make a psychological standoff with other groups probable even before issues are faced or events force their interaction. A concept such as human rights tends to be defined by the norms of "human-ness" prevailing in one's own culture. This, of course, becomes part of the psychological explanation for the extremes in brutality exhibited in more lethal ethnic conflicts.

Logically, then, analyzing any given case of ethnic conflict starts with an inquiry into cultural content in greater detail than is our usual practice, since these details become critical as the starting point for interacting with other groups in a conflict situation.

2

Second Problem Area: Sorting Out Ethnic Identities and Calculating Their Strength

If our first problem area considered ethnicity as a matter of ethnic culture, *this next problem area considers ethnicity in terms of the people involved: Who is to be included, when, and by what rules of loyalty?*

When problems develop into ethnic conflicts, the on-the-ground question is where the lines of group identity will be drawn. Just who will rally to an ethnic cause? When will people think as ethnicity would dictate and when according to the norms of some larger social or national sense of belonging? It seems obvious enough that without a tendency to choose sides by ethnic identity, there would be no ethnic conflict, and that where identities are weak, any conflict will be pursued with less single-minded ethnic determination. But there are many variables in the way that ethnic identities work out. Sometimes they apply rigorously, even to risking death before compromise. In other instances they are diffused into the multiple identities that people may hold or into a sense of belonging to a more encompassing civic or pluralistic society. An individual might, for example, be a member of an ethnic group at home and speak the ethnic language with close friends, be a citizen of a large nation when thinking about public affairs, and work for a multinational company. First loyalty would depend on the issue and the circumstances.

In larger perspective, it can be argued that this question of identity has importance well beyond the realm of local disputes. Note that the way people think of their membership in an ever more closely knit world community has much to do with our ability to solve collective problems in an interdependent world society. Much of our difficulty, on the one hand, is that economic and political institutions have to operate at a very much expanded scale of interdependence, while for most people the largest sense of social universe with which they can identify and extend the kind of loyalty needed to support such collective efforts remains, variously, the clan, tribe, local ethnic group, or nation at best. Unfortunately, many of today's problems do not come packaged that way.

There are relatively few genuine world citizens. People tend to collaborate most effectively to solve their immediate problems rather than abstract collective ones. For most global issues, this sense of what is to be considered "our" problem is not large enough to match the nature of the reality that is to be confronted. For many nation-states, there is not enough of a critical mass of citizens who habitually identity with their national-level society to make national-level institutions work. The nation-building problems of newly independent states, whose boundaries were often created with little concern for any national-level identities, are familiar to readers. It is worth recalling the words said to have been delivered before the Risorgimento after the modern state of Italy was brought into being: "Having made Italy, we must now make Italians." The concept of "national interest" and civic society is more elusive than those socialized in Western democracies often imagine.

This larger problem will be discussed further in a subsequent chapter. For the moment, it is important to note that establishing the outer limits of who is included as "one of us" has much to do with choice of strategy and the appeal of suggested solutions when ethnic conflict is addressed.

Still, we recognize that it is difficult to make accurate analytical estimates of binding identities when in the modern world ethnic identities often are not clear-cut. We may even use the term "ethnic conflict" too facilely. In cases where contending groups are clearly distinct in their subcultures, overlapping identities will often exist for many people, and in cases of modernization and rapid social and cultural change, their sense of who they are may well be submerged into their loyalty to a larger national society.

However, in international practice the difficulty usually is not only a matter of trying to establish where ethnic identity lines are drawn, but also of trying to understand why, in a given set of circumstances, people opt to adhere so fiercely to one of their various possible identities. The question comes up in many places. It poses a problem in social and political analysis in the United States, the "melting pot" society. When, for example, is it necessary to think of an Hispanic American as a special kind of American with special problems, and when as just an ordinary American? It is often a key social issue in cases of rapid urbanization and industrialization where folk societies with their traditional cultures are melding into larger, more secular national societies. For the individual, the identity question becomes: When am I an Ibo and when a Nigerian? When a Cebuano and

ino? Or, more generically, when am I a loyal
the ways of my village, and when am I a
cosmopolitan city person, or even part of an international
society that enjoys world standards of living, a globally
oriented lifestyle, and possibly an international culture?

The reality is that a large portion of the world's population today wears some degree of multiple identity. Industrialization with its diversified work settings, for example, cuts across ethnic lines to provide new norms of
association. At the least, with exposure to international
media, one's sense of identity loses some of its clear definition around the edges as alternate ideas and values
enter one's awareness and as one's social horizons expand. The problem is compounded when one contrasts
identity manifested on an intellectual level with identity
on an emotional or "gut" level. It is more probable that
people can identify with larger circles of society on an
intellectual level, especially where there is no conflict in
the offing. When emotions and sentiments are aroused,
it goes the other way.

So again for the practitioner the question becomes
why, as conflicts develop, will a particular identity take
precedence, and why will that identity be sustained with
such emotional vigor and sense of antagonism against
perceived enemies? By what process do social, political,
or economic issues become ethnic issues, with solutions
demanded that will satisfy an ethnically compatible logic?
Or, more dramatically, how is it that ethnic identity will
be drawn so closely that hardship and even death will be
blindly placed on the line and enemies will come to lose
all definition as human beings with "human rights" and
therefore be subjected to the kind of violence and brutality so often experienced?

Ethnic identity is, then, itself a state of mind, a
mindset. Once triggered, it supplies the cultural lens for
perceiving events and issues, and it becomes the con-

trolling frame of reference or starting point for reasoning about them. The usual objective in field operations is to get people to rise above their most narrow identities in the interest not only of their own well-being, but that of some larger society, national or international—which brings one to consider more carefully the psychological nature of group identity itself. How does the individual come to draw lines around a particular recognized social group and come to think in terms of "us" and "them"? And why might the dividing lines change from time to time and occasion to occasion?

ET

Factors Affecting Strength of Group Identity

Among the many factors that will tend to strengthen one's sense of ethnic identity and reinforce the patterns of perception that run along ethnic lines, the following stand out.[1]

Language

This is an obvious component of identity and feelings of exclusiveness. Does the group in question have its own language? Does it ordinarily use it? Do all members speak it? Is it used as a matter of pride and social dignity? Does it have a literature of consequence? How exclusively do people speak it? Do they also speak another language? (The person who is bilingual would hold some degree of bicultural identity, of course.)

---

[1] For a more penetrating review of the social psychology of group identity, see Daniel Druckman, "Nationalism, Patriotism, and Group Loyalty: A Social Psychological Perspective," *Mershon International Studies Review* 38, Supplement no. 1 (April 1944): 43-68.

We need to note that the significance of language goes beyond the mechanics of communication. Given the intimate association between language and culture, differing languages will tend to pose separate worlds of subjective meaning, nuance, sentiment, and even models for thinking and reasoning. The impact of this on identity could be great indeed.

The tie-in between language and a group's view of reality and its implicit philosophy is a much-studied subject in anthropology, linguistics, and psychology. The significance of this for in-group versus out-group feelings goes well beyond what would be expected when we think of language differences as being simply options for communicating the same thing: it suggests that there is a difference in subjective culture to be communicated. With a gap in nuances, there will be more of a sense of social distance between people speaking differing languages, or even with people speaking the same language as a second language. Within the mother tongue, the comfort and confidence level is high, the anxiety level low. In consequence, the *affective* worlds of two languages will not equate easily; poetry, for example, often does not translate well. Sentiments can be quite culture-specific; you cannot really separate the feelings that go with being *simpatico* from the cultures that go with speaking Spanish. To add to it, the affective or emotional dimension of communication also depends on customs of nonverbal communication which are ethnic-specific. How could one be Italian without Italian gestures?

Further, with language, both oral and written, comes a full range of legend and myth, folklore, group memory, an educational process, and humor that is shared easily and naturally within the language group. Thus a language comes to constitute a psychological world of ideas and outlooks that is internalized as an insider's psychological world.

Therefore, it is rarely possible for an outsider to fully penetrate the mindsets of an ethnic group without acquiring a genuine command of that group's language. Interestingly, in the sense that a language is so psychologically close to the "us" versus "them" divide, some groups, the Japanese and Koreans, for instance, discourage the outsider's efforts to learn their language *too* well. It somehow seems overly intrusive.

In sum, in analyzing ethnic conflict, attention to language has a significance that goes well beyond recognizing a simple communication barrier. Language is an integral part of both a sense of identity and the mindsets that go with it.

Ethics and Religion

These do not always go together, but there is good reason to pay as much attention as we do to religion as a key element in ethnicity and, therefore, in ethnic identity. One will identify most closely and feel most comfortable with other people who believe the same things and define the world about them with the same implicit philosophy. And when these beliefs are fundamental to one's underlying sense of what is natural, right, and ethical, religious identity quickly translates into a basis for separating those who are deemed to be naturally human from all those other people who are not only aliens, but aliens in the most fundamental way. In close proximity, a religious divide itself can often almost guarantee an uncompromising sense of opposing identity: Hindus and Muslims in India, Catholics and Protestants in Ireland, to name only two cases.

Hence, the attention we pay to religious and ethical systems for their role in helping people define who they are and how they differ from other people is logical. The ideas that go with a religious philosophy come to be the building blocks of mindsets, and most especially the mindsets relating to social relations. They are not easily put aside, as we will see in the next chapter when we discuss problems of intransigence.[2]

It is also useful to note that in the normal course of being internalized, ethical conceptions and religious beliefs tend to develop *emotional* overtones which add to a sense of social alienation when dealing with people whose ethical systems and religious persuasions are different. It is hard to be objective, or conclude that it is all relative, when your deeply held codes are violated. Even in routine behavior, a degree of social distance can be injected. If, for example, religion sanctions what people eat or what clothing they wear—or do not wear—empathy can be reduced. Modesty and food taboos tend to be emotional matters. Therefore, with religious differences, the stage is set for emotional reactions even before the issues in a confrontation are taken up.

The role of religion is already well recognized in dealing with ethnic conflict, of course, and we are painfully aware of its consequences. Both sides can be expected to appeal to the Almighty of their ethnic choice for divine assistance. And all kinds of mayhem can be perpetrated with religious and ethical justification. However, our main concern here is religion as a contributing factor in ethnic identity. In this regard, several questions stand out as particularly germane.

How homogeneous is the ethnic group as a religious community? Does everyone who speaks the language and follows the customs adhere to or recognize the same religious or ethical base? Are there schisms or deep differ-

---

[2] For a basic statement of the role that belief systems play in group outlooks, see David Little, "Belief, Ethnicity, and Nationalism," *Nationalism and Ethnic Politics* 1, no. 2 (Summer 1995): 284-30l. For the way that religion gets mixed with other factors, see his *Sri Lanka: The Invention of Enmity* (Washington, DC: United States Institute of Peace Press, 1994).

ences in adherence? This is a fundamental problem in making identities coalesce in Israel. Is the group's religion unique to it, or is it shared by outside groups with whom one might identify to a degree? For example, being Catholic in Ireland provides a Catholic identity beyond Ireland, or being Muslim in Bosnia provides an identity—although perhaps a tenuous one in this case—in the larger Muslim world.

How pure or unadulterated is religion as a belief system? Or to what degree have essential beliefs and ethical standards been eroded in the face of modernization or the inroads of other belief systems? To what degree does religion still supply basic values and a worldview even in the absence of dogmatic belief or adherence to strict religious practice? We note that there is a strong Jewish ethos based on religion that goes into many Jewish mindsets, even including those of nonpracticing Jews. The same is true for Catholics and Protestants, and it is well recognized in Confucian societies.

What kind of worldview is implicit in the religion in question? That is, what ways of thinking are built into religious systems that will affect conceptions of such matters as the nature of the universe, time, the environment and the individual's relation to it, social relations, authority, or human responsibilities versus those of the Divine? And how much do the idea patterns of religion become the basic assumptions for other institutions such as law, education, government, commerce, the family, or as the rationale for daily life? This latter is a loaded question, for in the way that cultures develop as systems with the parts seeking consistency with other parts, the basic themes that characterize a given religion will tend to be themes that have to be accommodated in other institutions, multiplying religion's effect. In Islamic communities, for example, even banks have to make some adjustment to religious precepts about charging interest!

Which specific beliefs are the critically sensitive and emotional ones, that is, the ones that when attacked will most likely trigger threatened identity reactions and lead to outrage?

To what extent do religious leaders automatically become the recognized leaders of the ethnic group itself?

Other aspects of the religion and strength-of-identity connection may occur to the reader. The point is that, because underlying philosophy and ethical systems are so central to group cohesion, they are fundamental to calculating strength of identity.

Being Assigned an Identity by a Larger Society

How exclusively one feels one's ethnic identity is much affected by the nature of the larger society's structure and the degree to which the ethnic group is relegated to a closely defined position within it. Being socially isolated in one way or another in a larger society reinforces one's separate identity, whether that position is advantageous, as in the case of a ruling ethnic elite, or disadvantageous, as it is with an ethnic group which is considered inferior in social status, which is restricted in economic activity, or which is oppressed politically. The degree of rigidity in such separation again affects the "us" versus "them" quality of social relations. Indeed, when the social wall is high and institutionalized, the very thought of identifying with something other than one's own ethnic group is inhibited. The status of Indian groups in much of the history of Latin America is illustrative; a Guatemalan Indian, for example, would have only taken on an unrealistic psychological burden in trying to identify with Ladinos (mestizos), much less the Criollos of European lineage, and vice versa. In India, caste went a long way to define identity; one simply could not identify with a differing segment of the society. This problem persists to some extent today. When social and cultural change takes place in these aspects of social structure, the task of calculating the strength of ethnic identity becomes much more complex.

Further, in areas of former colonial administration, how various ethnic groups fit into colonial society may have had consequences for postcolonial times, especially when one group had been assigned special economic or administrative roles. For example, today's Sinhalese–Tamil conflict in Sri Lanka seems to have had its roots partially in British colonial administration when the minority Tamils enjoyed many such advantages.

In working with specific individuals in ethnic conflict areas, identities assigned internally within an ethnic group on the one hand, and externally by the larger society on the other, might present enough inconsistencies to create confusion for outsiders who want to understand how their counterparts see themselves. An elite status that goes, for example, with wealth, education, or professional position in the larger society might cut across one's status as an ethnic group member. Senegal seems to be such a case. Depending on the issue, wealth and position—being involved in modern urban or public affairs, for instance—often count most regardless of group identity. But in community life or politics, or in business or work relationships, ethnicity counts. Reporting from experience in Burundi, an American specialist working in a development program noted something similar. In the case of her local team, composed of both Tutsis and Hutus, ethnicity was mostly muted. Still, the Hutu team coleader always sat in the back of their official vehicle with the rest of the Hutus despite professional team-leader status.

History and Its Events
Contribute to Sense of Identity

We are well accustomed to reviewing an ethnic group's history—whether heroic or demeaning—in any quest for understanding conflict scenarios. And we already recognize that a consciousness of history and its salient events goes a long way toward establishing a sense of identity. So we add history to the list of basic factors establishing in-group ways of thinking and perceiving. This would not need elaboration here except for the need to stress the often underappreciated significance of history *as actually remembered*.

We need to distinguish between two different kinds of history. On the one hand we have history as fact, as best we can establish it; scholars and academics rightfully pride themselves on establishing order and objectivity in the record of the past.

But this is not the history that necessarily goes into identity mindsets, for *that* "history" is psychologically processed. It is history as it is remembered and subjectively understood that counts. And it is this history that becomes part of the ethos that, as a dimension of culture, is learned, shared, and transmitted in group life. But we tend to be less analytically persistent in trying to capture this kind of history even though it is the operative history when conflict is to be understood. Beyond what actually happened, *subjective* history—or if you wish, mindset history—includes legend and myth, heroes that are larger than life, successes that are exaggerated, villains that are demonized, and events that are remembered selectively or that never took place at all. The more dramatic and emotionally laden, the more this history-as-remembered adds to strength of identity.

While people regularly look to heroes and epic deeds to lend a note of pride to their group ethos, ethnic identity can also revolve around experienced martyrdom, persecution, and unrevenged loss. These kinds of negative elements can be an exceptionally strong factor in group identity. Armenian self-perceptions as victims, as well as those of Jews, for example, are to the point. In the Balkans, this kind of culturally reinforced identity is common. Again, Paul Mojzes, in explaining the forces that fuel conflict in the former Yugoslavia, captures it well in one of his chapter headings: "The Destructive Use of Memory."[3] That is, a history of suffering as remembered, with all its collectively shared emotional charge, serves to perpetuate group identity. It is used as a support for group solidarity both in the normal course of events and, in the Bosnia conflagration, for example, by the leadership with the intention to trigger the kind of group response that in this case led to disaster.

Unfortunately, we tend to be wary of using such psychological "fact" as hard data. These items tend to get set aside as irrational and therefore less germane to serious negotiating and conflict management. Subjective history and objective history may, of course, coincide, but the point is that capturing the essence of the way that a given identity is programmed requires a close look at the subjective forces that drive it. One cannot gain an empathetic perspective otherwise.

While we list subjective history as critical in understanding identity, care is also required in fine-tuning its significance. For myths can fade; new generations may hold less compelling memories; new history dilutes the old. Establishing the precise role played by subjective history in a current generation's sense of ethnic identity is a particularly demanding exercise, as such trends have to be estimated.

The Culture's Own Provisions for Preserving Identity

Ethnic cultures differ in the degree that special or exclusive identity is a central theme of the culture itself. For example, it would be hard to understand Jewish identity

---

[3] Paul Mojzes, *Yugoslavian Inferno*, 45.

apart from the way that Jewish culture insists that it is special. The themes are prominent and have served the group well as Jews scattered over the world and into a wide variety of host societies: the special quality of Jews as a people, the high value placed on a geographical place of origin and on a continuing orientation toward it, a religion that emphasizes the idea of a chosen and unique people apart from others, plus a cumulative memory of hostility from other groups. These pervade the Judaic ethos. It is, in sum, a *culture* of special identity. Japanese culture also emphasizes the exclusiveness of being Japanese and includes themes that range from a stress on the value of the group itself to an outlook that categorizes all outsiders as *gaijin*. This is so strong that Japanese who live abroad suffer significant identity problems when they come home; their Japaneseness is suspect.

American cultural patterns are more open as far as reinforcing identity is concerned. The United States began, after all, as an inclusive, pluralistic, multigroup society which valued the individual and individual achievement. It was assumed that all outsiders would want to be Americans, or at least be like Americans! The cultural theme, then, is inclusiveness, at least in concept. It was the mindset that supported immigration as the right and proper way to expand the society, as long as the immigrant was ready to acculturate and adopt an American identity.

So a search for identity-reinforcing mechanisms that are incorporated into the culture itself can go a long way in explaining identity and its strengths. Among the questions to pursue in this search: How pervasively is value placed on the group itself and its well-being as opposed to the individual? How is a sense of special common origin treated in tradition and custom? Who are the heroes, and is it easy for everyone to empathize with them? Do myths, sentiments, dreams, customs, and traditions tend to stress special identity? What are the symbols of ethnicity? How does the culture define outsiders and what are the patterned ways for dealing with them—be suspicious and stay on guard, or honor them and extend hospitality?

Identity Reinforcement

We conclude this short and somewhat arbitrary list of factors that bear on strength of ethnic identity by calling attention to external factors which *reinforce* identity, or which set in bolder relief the self-images and images of the "other" that pertain so directly to the psychology of conflict. We call attention here to three types of reinforcing factors.

The nature of conflict issues and events themselves can trigger otherwise latent or generally benign identity awareness if they relate to critical group concerns. The violent incident with ethnic overtones or the political or economic crisis that seems to make an ethnic group a victim are obvious examples. When in the course of political upheaval such stability as might have gone with being part of a larger functioning social system is lost, ethnic group membership becomes a fallback position, the last-resort source of security in troubled times. Lacking other options for a predictable and caring social universe, one's ethnic identity becomes all the more important. The breakup of the Soviet Union and especially of Yugoslavia, with the questions suddenly posed as to who would govern whom, how political divisions would be made, and who would enjoy authority and advantage, were dramatic examples. If in such a process the group acquires enemies, and especially enemies of another ethnicity, the ways of one's own group, in mirror image, are morally validated and belonging to it becomes more emotionally reassuring. The point is that events can suddenly make ethnic identity the critical element and lead the people involved to perceive everything that is occurring through an ethnic lens. And the genius of conflict resolution strategy, of course, is to avoid creating new events or articulating issues in ways that further freeze identity at an uncompromising ethnic level.

The *media can be a critical factor* in triggering a sense of identity by the information they present, the subjective meaning conveyed, and the dramatic appeal by which they gain attention. The potential for casting issues in ethnic terms and for dramatizing ethnic interests or anxieties is obvious, especially when specifically used for this purpose. This element has been seen as so important in Malaysia that the government, with considerable public consensus, holds media in close check as the tensions within the national society among Malays, Chinese, and Indian ethnic groups are concerns for everyone. In Malaysia's short history as an independent nation, a flash point has on occasion been reached by media presenting problems in ethnic terms—and with violent effect. On the other hand, media can be a factor in defusing narrower loyalties and enhancing national identity. One recalls the way that the international press descended on the Philippines during the toppling of Ferdinand Marcos. As Filipinos, often of many contesting identities, together did something heroic and praiseworthy in the full light of international publicity, the idea of being Filipino took on an enhanced aura.

The third is *the way that political leadership deals with ethnicity* in the process of contesting for power and influence. The ethnic dimension can come into play in both directions of the leadership function: On the one hand, ethnic interests in a given situation demand leadership; on the other, leadership can use the ethnic card to its own advantage. In any case, leadership can be a major factor in determining the degree to which ethnic identity will coalesce around developing issues. On the negative side, in his propaganda strategy Hitler appealed to the emotions that went with Aryan identity. Serbian President Slobodan Milosevic has been singled out especially for setting off the disintegration of Yugoslavia by playing to Serbian identity in his reach for power.[4] Yasir Arafat probably would have had to be invented if he had not come along to appeal to a latent sense of Palestinian identity in the conflict with the Israelis.

---

[4] For example, former U.S. Ambassador to Yugoslavia Warren Zimmerman makes this case in his *Origins of a Catastrophe: Yugoslavia and Its Destroyers* (New York: Times Books, 1996).

3

Third Problem Area: Explaining Intransigence

Coping with intransigence is perhaps the most difficult problem imposed on the mediator and negotiator as ways are sought to defuse ethnic conflict. The solution thought reasonable is rejected. Compromise is not appealing. The pain suffered in active conflict seems to be more bearable than the best terms proposed in settlement. A peaceful solution as an objective seems to hold a higher priority for the outside mediator than for the participants pursuing their adamant views of the issues. And even after a conflict appears to be resolved, intransigence can linger on in complying with any compromise.

For all one's attempt to empathize, the intransigence encountered frustrates and tends to defy explanation. The mind*sets* at work are just that—very, very set! At the start there is intransigence just in agreeing to meet with the opposing side. Then the "facts" of the conflict cannot be established; each party has fixed beliefs in this regard that will not yield to evidence, regardless of the objectivity of the source. Conceptions of what constitutes agreeable solutions seem to be set in cement. And little virtue is seen in compromise per se.

The mediation process is also plagued by misperception and, most difficult of all, misattribution of motives, as mindsets are projected to explain why parties to the conflict, or even the mediators, are doing what they are doing. It is hard to turn around misattributions of motives. As in working with a computer, when a given program is engaged, the way that new information is processed is preestablished. The only way to get around it is to modify the programming or plug in a new one, which is not easily done in human computers.

The objective, then, is to anticipate intransigence, understand its sources and dynamics for the ethnic group in question, judge its firmness or malleability, and adapt one's strategy accordingly. This does not necessarily mean yielding to intransigence; it may mean a more careful calibration of the pressure to be exerted if that is the choice, or recasting a solution to work around whatever the sticking point of the intransigence is.

The possible sources of intransigence for any specific ethnic group would seem to be limitless, and all the considerations discussed in the last two sections apply. However, we might narrow the objective of the search by trying to identify what might be thought of as conflict-specific "stress points," the deeply held ideas or implicit assumptions that, for any particular conflict, would be critical. For example, the firm Zionist belief in the moral sanctity of a "Land of Israel" would be a clear example of a "stress point," as it is a central mindset factor in Middle East mediation efforts and one on which Israelis and Palestinians obviously and deeply disagree. But it is a stress point that requires examination in its detail. On the Israeli side it constitutes something of a dividing line in public thinking, as those very fixed in their emphasis on a 3000-year-old geographical tradition insist on settlements on the West Bank such as those in Hebron, while secular Jews can conceive of compromise in the interest of peaceful co-occupation of the area. This split in degree of intransigence was put to the test in Shimon Perez's electoral defeat in 1996 after he continued to move toward compromises despite a new round of terrorist attacks that reminded the public of its vulnerability and strengthened the resolve of the territorial purists.

Thus, somewhat as an engineer has to anticipate the stress points in constructing a bridge, so does the analyst of an ethnic conflict. Which mindset factors will turn out to be most critical and have to be taken most into account? This makes the search more difficult, for stress points embedded in mindsets are not always stated or apparent. Again, specialists who concentrate on the areas and cultures involved can be helpful; in fact, as we noted earlier, one of their justifications for being in the analytical business should be their ability to spot such points of probable intransigence.

However, as one often has to be one's own area and culture specialist, or at least be prepared to set the priorities in seeking information and advice, it might be helpful here to present some of the typical psychocultural sources of intransigence, particularly those associated with "deep culture."

Deep Culture

Some mindset elements are more important than others. Looking for an underlying deep culture is an approach that derives from the study and analysis of cross-cultural interaction. It supplies a useful framework for our discussion here. As opposed to cultural elements that can be easily seen and talked about, or "surface" culture, deep culture addresses what is behind it all. To elaborate somewhat on the culture and personality concepts proposed earlier, it calls attention to the *fundamental* ideas and implicit assumptions that one absorbs in the process of growing up in a society and being enculturated into the ways of thinking normal to it. It supplies the most essential elements from which mindsets are constructed. It is "deep" in two ways.

First, it is deep because it is learned out-of-awareness and seems natural and universal. So natural, in fact, that people are not aware that they face the world with a particularly unique set of value orientations, notions about the forces of nature, assumptions about relations among people, sense of cause and effect, and so forth. For example, for people in many parts of Asia, well-structured reciprocal obligation to other people is a common-sense value, learned and absorbed in growing up and taken for granted. It is part of their core value system. They would feel at a loss without these obligations and would be inclined to view the Westerner's relaxed attitude toward binding mutual obligations strange if not bizarre.

It is also deep in that these key mindset components tend to apply as implicit assumptions across the board as an underlying rationale for all the group's customs and institutions, thus supplying a thread of consistency and mutual compatibility for the cultural system. They become the variables which if changed would produce repercussions all down the line. If, for example, one assumes, as a given culture might prescribe, that humans are powerless subjects of the forces of nature, a sense of fatalism becomes a starting point for thinking about planting crops, the death of children, one's position in the social structure, and the potential benefits of playing the lottery where some superior force may bring good luck. But a starting assumption that humans can and should intervene in the forces of nature leads to achievement motivation, scientific agriculture, an egalitarian social structure where people strive for position, and a judicial system that assigns blame when things go wrong. As another example, concepts of honor or loyalty can be deeply held and can differ by culture. This often affects the rationale for specific conduct in the course of ethnic conflict. We mentioned the lost-cause syndrome earlier; it can become a part of deep culture along with a value placed on revenge itself.

Deep culture thus has a lot to do with intransigence. For these basic starting points underlying mindsets come to be ingrained and unquestioned if culture has done its job in supplying a design for meeting life's problems and keeping the many parts of a culture consistent and integrated.

Intransigence, then, is to be expected when these building blocks of deep culture are challenged. Culture seeks consistency; it rejects that which disturbs consistency even when the proposal seems well reasoned and objective to the mediator.

Religion, both as institutionalized doctrine and as a more general system of customary philosophy, provides an obvious starting point for exploring deep culture. As a supplier of ways of thinking that are prone to clash in ethnic confrontations, its importance can hardly be overstated. As in its role in cementing ethnic identities discussed in the previous section, religious belief stands out as a core factor in fueling intransigence. What makes it so central is the fact that it fulfills a rather special function for humans in that it supplies them with a way of organizing thinking about the types of basic life concerns that cannot be fathomed by one's own empirical observation: the forces of the universe, life and death, disease, fortune and misfortune, the purpose of life. And for these "mental customs" to be useful, the individual has to absorb them all as a matter of faith and belief, as ways of thinking not to be questioned. (Systems of thought other than religion might serve, or come to serve, the same function; science would be an example, but of course, it also would have to be believed. We note that virtually all cultures supply explanations for the origin of humans. Usually religious explanations came first. Hence the problem posed by the theory of evolution derived from scientific inquiry and the "cognitive dissonance" that it produces!)

Thus we find that religion, and the patterns of thinking that go with it in each culture, occupy a central position in the psychocultural system by which mindsets are generated and intransigence is programmed. When its adherents have to suffer those who do not believe the same way, whether deviants in their own society or outsiders who deviate en masse, contrary outlooks are a threat to that which is fundamental; the stage is set for sticking to one's mindsets. When religious belief includes a mandate to proselytize, intransigence turns into aggression, as it did in the Crusades and various instances of Islamic jihad, and in milder forms in Western missionary activity.

Further, by their function in supplying meaning and purpose, these religious and philosophical orientations also tend to supply the basis for evaluating what is moral, right, and acceptable, even human. While a close connection between ethics and religion as understood in Western Protestantism is not necessarily paralleled in other cultures—sin and guilt ethics in contrast with the shame ethics of many less individualistic societies—the moral basis for human behavior will usually fit, as norms, into a package consistent with the thought patterns embedded in religion. In sum, it becomes immoral to tolerate behavior deviations too facilely.

Beyond the basic idea patterns institutionalized in religion, other culturally established assumptions and values are to be found in deep culture. For example, in American society, the intrinsic worth of the individual tends to take priority as a starting assumption for people going about their life activities and, therefore, is infused in the logic of their institutions. That is, Americans generally value individualism as contrasted with placing a primary value on the group—to which the individual is left subordinate, as in Japan and in many traditional societies. Saying that Americans value the individual, with the egalitarianism and achievement motivation that go with it, might seem to be too strong a generalization when glaring exceptions can be cited. Yet this is a prominent theme or underlying programming principle of American culture, and it gains importance as a central value because it supplies an element of logic for many other aspects of the culture: social relations, the economic system, religion, education, the family structure, even humor. As implicit mindset components, such basic themes help explain why people so often talk past each other in cross-cultural encounters; they are reflecting the programming of differing deep cultures. A stress point is demonstrated in that such differences produce exceptionally important consequences for the cross-cultural interaction process.

Such is the theory. Clearly identifying the aspects of deep culture that are in play in a given ethnic conflict situation requires a certain amount of cultural analysis. And this is further complicated as cultures change, peoples mix and hold multiple identities—and often suffer conflicting value systems within their own psyches. Yet the inquiry is fundamental if one is to understand the kind of unbending perception and reasoning often exhibited in ethnic confrontation.

Mindsets Fit into Cultural Systems and Are Thus Reinforced

Several considerations for anticipating intransigence follow from the above discussion. One is the generalization that *the more a given idea pattern serves across the board as an essential part of the logic of a society's institutions, the more it resists compromise or alteration.*

It is useful to think of a culture as being something like a jigsaw puzzle. Its "pieces" are interlocked; the whole puzzle fits together, with its central themes—the items of deep culture noted above—supplying the basic design of the picture that is achieved when the puzzle is assembled. The parts of a culture make sense only in the context of the larger system. This is basic cultural anthropology. If a part is removed, it spoils the picture. And if that part is one of the well-established bits of customary thinking that is carried in the design across the board, the system in turn makes it harder to give it up. If, for example, seeking revenge or thinking in terms of "an eye for an eye and a tooth for a tooth" is held as a conventional way to redress wrong, and if it is also institutionalized in family traditions as a matter of upholding honor, is an expected subject for regulation in legal institutions, is provided for in religious sanctions, and is honored as a theme in literature and folklore, there is a reinforcement process at work that more forcefully sustains the thought pattern regarding revenge wherever it applies.

Or, put the other way around, the more that a given proposal for conflict resolution depends on applying an outsider's assumptions that do *not* seem consistent with the logic inherent in the ethnic group's cultural system, the less likely it will be that the proposal will be persuasive. You cannot simply put a new piece into the puzzle unless it is sustained by and meshes with existing themes.

The new idea will just not feel right. Hoping that a sense of "fair play"—from a British/American perspective—will support a proposed compromise is an example. The concept barely exists outside the English language. It would be a case of trying to insert a piece that fits well enough in one puzzle, but not another.

Followers May Expect a Leader to Be Intransigent

A special difficulty encountered in managing *ethnic* conflict in contrast to other kinds is that it is harder for the outsider to know who makes decisions and who actually leads, and then to anticipate actual role expectations. Formal title may mean little. The religious leader might be more important than the secular one; a traditional authority might be more influential that a bureaucratic one. For example, finding out who exercised the local, ethnically sanctioned role of conflict mediator was an important step in the Somalia intervention; often they were not the people who appeared in formal organizational charts, but village-level elders invisible to outsiders. As for national-level Somalian decision making, people operating from Western concepts of national-level government organizational charts had to deal with "clan leaders," a position description that would be vague to them at best. Thus a situation emerged in which leaders might be asked to rise above clan interests in ways that would make them act against the clan role expectations by which they exercised authority in the first place.

In any case, as leaders lead or representatives negotiate, their way of thinking about events and issues can be expected to be a function of their culturally generated conceptions of themselves as they play out their role expectations as leaders. Anthropologists speak of the "press of culture." This is a clear example, for expected role behavior involves mindsets shared by the group and the leader. It is an especially interesting matter when leaders are cosmopolitan in outlook and are intellectually persuadable in negotiation. But when the chips are down, they have to reflect group expectations. And intransigence can still be expected as leaders consciously or unconsciously project the idea patterns *expected* of them, whether it be beliefs regarding the issue, suspicions of other groups or parties, animosities, or even rhetorical styles.

The problem of intransigence is greater when a leader holds authority by virtue of charismatic qualities as contrasted with legal or bureaucratic credentials. Especially in situations in which ethnic groups are contesting established authority, the emerging leader has to be someone who in personality embodies the emotions and aspirations of the ethnic cause, is the one who can articulate group concerns, is the hero or the one who has earned leadership in the drama of conflict itself. The charismatic leader's asset is the ability to reflect the mindsets of the group, usually with added emotional impact. This, in effect, becomes another way in which the ethnic view of the conflict is locked in; compromising on it would be a matter of compromising leadership credentials.

An effective international negotiator well understands a counterpart's need to play out local expectations in role behavior, of course, and exotic instances become part of the lore of the negotiating and mediating fraternity. Supplying the luxury car as a symbol of importance, allowing the local leader to take some of the credit when relief goods are dispensed, the ride in the helicopter, praise in the press release, or deferring to a leader's need to "take care of" key supporters all have something to do with defusing intransigence. Dealing with an incompetent or corrupt leader who has to appear competent and statesmanlike is a decidedly challenging task for the outsider with differing expectations for leadership role behavior.

Apparent Cosmopolitanism Can Be Misleading

Beliefs and attitudes ingrained earliest tend to be the most persistent. We are aware that personality development is much affected by early learning processes. What one learns, and how one learns to think about it, become well established by the age of five or six during the time that one is absorbing language and the built-in conceptualizations that go with it. While new experience and further learning may well make considerable modifications in patterns of thinking, there is a progression that builds on a base of idea patterns that is not easily undone. Mindsets build on mindsets, and fundamental changes do not normally occur.

This also applies to ethnic groups in the aggregate, to the acculturation process in a society, and to the ethos or what we think of as the "national character" of the ethnic group. (And it applies to the outsider practitioner, of course.) Culture works best if its norms are internalized early and firmly. In consequence, *intransigence can be most expected when the idea patterns drawn upon in the process of perceiving issues are those learned early when people were growing up in their ethnic environment.* This is consistent with the deep-culture concept. What is learned later is less deeply embedded in the psychic matrix; it is more likely to be subject to change. But even when later experience supersedes that which has been incorporated in early life, it does not erase it. That early attachment tends to persist. In consequence, a note of caution is suggested for the conflict manager who tends to be impressed with a counterpart's university degrees earned abroad. The way of thinking that people carry with them does not start with the university, it starts in childhood; and in the context of ethnic conflict, that early ethnic part will weigh heavily in the psyches of those involved no matter how much education they have or where it was obtained.

What is learned early is especially germane when the whole subject of prejudice is considered. As we know, it is hard to talk people out of their prejudices. Or, if intellectually persuaded, persuasion at the emotional and affective level is rarely complete. Latent prejudices persist, and conflict itself tends to draw out such feelings with the emotions of the confrontation often reinforcing them. We note especially the cases of groups living peacefully in interethnic proximity with their prejudices held in latent readiness to surface when conflict erupts. Again, the case of the Balkans is to the point. The prejudices that people there learn early in their lives are much the same as those which children have learned early for generations. What was added in education during the years of socialist cosmopolitanism, possibly in another language, worked like a veneer while communist institutions were in place, but left the underlying outlooks largely intact to surface when communist rule collapsed and it was one ethnic group against another.

In general, this source of intransigence, while often recognized, is usually given insufficient stress in diagnosing the dynamics of a confrontation and judging the prospects for resolution. In the United States, prejudice has a bad name, of course, as it goes against a democratic ethic, and the emphasis has been more on changing or defusing prejudice than on objectively probing its source in the subcultures of the national society. Carried overseas, this approach becomes superficial. Looking at prejudice in a new place requires an ethnically specific analysis in each case if critical prejudices are to be understood in the kind of detail needed for addressing them. While it sounds counterproductive, empathizing with prejudice is a fine art, and a necessary one in ethnic conflicts that are foreign to the observer.

Calculating Probable Resistance to Persuasion

Finally, how does one calculate how *much* intransigence can be expected from the mindset factors we have considered above? How serious or deeply embedded is a particular belief, value, fixed idea, or philosophical orientation? The problem is similar to that posed in evaluating the significance of a public opinion poll. It is one thing to tally *what* people think; it is another to know how *strongly* or adamantly they think it. Two initial factors that affect resistance to persuasion come to mind.

First, there is the question of how much emotional charge or subjective feeling is involved in a confrontation. We know that emotions become a heavy ingredient in intransigence. Here we enter the psychic realm of love and sentiment, of fear and hatred. While in this text we are not prepared to analyze emotional processes as a field of inquiry per se, emotional charge must still be factored in as a key item in the intransigence formula. Whether positive or negative, emotions add a dimension that goes well beyond an objective description of *what* people think and believe. Hatred is not simply a prejudice, but prejudice with the adrenaline added! Emotion adds a driving force. As an extreme, mass murder is a mindset run amok. The subject thus invites using the very considerable contributions of psychologists in understanding conflict behavior, whether it is ethnic or not.

Second, one needs to take into account the *extent* to which particular ideas or beliefs have come to dominate an entire system of ethnic thinking, have disproportionately taken precedence as controlling assumptions in a wide range of group institutions and affairs, and have the effect of locking out ways of thinking that are not compatible. From the outside point of view, this kind of thinking is often identified as fanaticism, but its relevance should not be underestimated nor dismissed for its seeming irrationality. The critical point is that such beliefs, by their rigidity and usually their emotional charge, force themselves into the perceptions of everything that the group faces in ethnic conflict situations. They become the key basis for perceptions, whatever the issue. Deviance within the ethnic group is not easily tolerated, and the mediator's appeal to "reason" has no audience. And extreme behavior, including terrorism or sacrificing life itself in suicide bombings, can come to be rationalized as reasonable strategy, both in the minds of those who carry it out and in the reasoning of the larger group where such action can be comfortably excused or even applauded.

Such exceptionally strong belief systems can have varied roots. Religion can be a source of these kinds of deeply embedded assumptions. Many believe Islamic fundamentalism to be such a source. Strong feelings and beliefs can also be carryovers from past conflicts such as those that took place during colonial times or independence movements. Or, in shorter-range perspective, they might be augmented by well-articulated hysteria generated by leaders or media. Usually they derive from a combination of sources.

Another question—beyond those related to the depth and rigidity of the idea patterns—is that of durability. In general, the longer mindset elements have been held and handed down as conventional wisdom, the more likely they will have become integrated into the design of the deep culture mentioned earlier. (In the words of the song from *South Pacific*, you learn to hate all the people your relatives hate.) And rigid beliefs are more durable the more broadly they are held in the ethnic population; mass beliefs have a reinforcing effect as they assume the validity of norms (groupthink) and make holding contrary beliefs seem like a deviation from group solidarity.

However, when not broadly held, they are likely to lack durability—which can prove to be an asset when mediation efforts call for compromise. Though dominating beliefs may be intense and are fanatically pursued in the drama of conflict, they can be short-lived if they really lack consistency with the larger web of thought patterns and concerns and fail to dominate the thinking of a wide range of group members. While the example comes from a somewhat different kind of conflict, it is interesting to note the relative ease with which Americans and Japanese lost the intensity of their reciprocal feelings and attitudes after World War II, or to observe how quickly the feeling that Americans were the enemy dissipated among the Vietnamese.

Judging the intensity and durability of critical outlooks is perhaps the most difficult part of making psychological estimates in diagnosing ethnic conflict. But it has everything to do with choosing strategies for containing conflict and for accurately anticipating how well solutions to conflicts will hold up.

4

Fourth Problem Area: Projecting Remedies for Conflict

Here, we ask how mindsets affect the way that strategies for managing conflicts work out after they are implemented. We are assuming, of course, that much of what has been said in previous sections will also apply to anticipating how well postconflict arrangements will fit into an ethnic conflict environment. After all, there is also a cross-cultural dimension to take into account as remedies for conflicts are projected across national and cultural lines. But in looking at postconflict arrangements, we need to focus on two additional mindset considerations that apply especially when mediators reflect the assumptions of Western democratic practice. One is differences in the way that a group's sense of what constitutes a *meaningful social universe* might be more or less inclusive. (This will require further explanation below.) The other is the degree to which the assumptions that underlie what we generally think of as a *civic society* can be used as the basis for conflict resolution.

Which brings us again to the reality that resolutions proposed for ethnic conflict tend to look very different from the perspective of one outside the conflict looking in than they do from that of people on the inside looking out. The key problem is that those who would prescribe remedies from the vantage point of the international community and of modern Western-style democracies will tend to *project* an expectation that narrow ethnic concerns should yield to interests of some larger, more encompassing society and that democratic processes and the norms of civic societies can provide more of a framework for addressing conflict than the view from the inside will allow.

This outsider's projection tends to assume, for example, that the mainstays of civic society—acceptance of some degree of pluralism, a contract conception of governmental authority, tolerance, and legitimacy established for both officials and policies by free and fair elections—will have a sanctity recognized by all. Refusal to budge beyond ethnic identity to resolve issues is seen then as a manifestation of social or political pathology. It assumes that the peoples in conflict *should* identify with some more encompassing society, at least in part of their social consciousness. This is especially true if the ethnic group is part of a recognized nation-state. Obstinacy, therefore, is seen as a break in a desirable evolution toward a larger national or perhaps even international identity, or as a backsliding from it.

This dilemma is so well stated by David Joel Steinberg in his discussion of the Philippines that it is worth quoting the two lead paragraphs of a chapter entitled "A Singular and a Plural Folk."

> One of the central dreams of all modern nation-states is the emergence of an integrated homogeneous society in which the citizenry shares a sense of common iden-

tity and an allegiance. The U.S. formulation of that aspiration is *e pluribus unum*. Nations exist through the delicate balance of the coercive power of the center and the willing compliance of the citizenry. If individuals or groups of individuals choose not to pledge their allegiance to the flag and to the nation for which it stands, that nation is unstable and must rely on the military or on the police power of the government for survival. Lincoln warned that "a house divided against itself cannot stand," and virtually every modern nation has experienced some form of civil war as the new patterns of allegiance and the priority of nationalist values have collided with older patterns. This reformulation of values, by which allegiance to the nation-state becomes paramount, is one of the central issues of twentieth-century history.

Virtually every subjugated colony has sought to define itself by waging an external struggle of liberation against the former imperial overlord and an internal struggle of reformulation of values against traditional, prenationalist value systems. Ethnicity, religious difference, linguistic identity, geographical and historical experience, different life experience, familial or clan obligation, kinship patterns—all of these represent priorities that are potentially antithetical to the nationalist dream. People will not think of themselves as Filipinos or Indonesians or Americans if they posit their religious, linguistic, geographical, or tribal values as being more central to their lives than their national-ist identity. Modern nationalism demands that the nation must be the prime alle-giance, the cause to which its citizens devote their loyalty and offer their lives.[1]

The analytical task then is to determine where the parties to a conflict are on a scale of expanding identities if one is to prescribe democratic processes or application of the kinds of conflict resolution approaches used in civic societies. This will vary considerably from case to case, with the prospects for resolution along democratic and civic society lines affected accordingly. Therefore, it is worth a bit of digression here to look more closely at the idea that expanding rings of group consciousness pose important implications for analyzing ethnic conflicts and for seeking solutions to them.

Broad and Narrow Social Horizons

Back to the idea of "social universe." Consider the way that people relate to the institutions they depend on so much in ordinary public life—government and its de-partments, courts, police, the media, social service agen-cies, and so forth. The question is what is one's psycho-logical relationship to them. On the one hand, these in-stitutions are structures that can be described and talked about. They can be discussed in terms of their rules and regulations, their standard operating procedures, the roles assigned to the people involved, and interrelationships with other institutions. Accordingly, from a structural point of view, such description explains how the public is organized, served, and ruled. In international affairs,

---

[1] David Joel Steinberg, *The Philippines: A Singular and a Plural Place*, 3d ed. (Boulder, CO: Westview Press, 1994), 37.

we tend to study institutions descriptively and comparatively in order to understand how one system differs from another structurally.

On the other hand, when all is going well, institutions work in reciprocal relationships with clients who identify with them and *expect* them to work. That is, they function because the public is more or less socialized into the idea that these are *their* institutions and that they operate as a normal state of affairs. Ideally, they are integrated into a compatible social system in which culture, values, and mindsets provide a supporting environment. Legal systems, for example, do not work simply by coercion, but by the fact that people agree and identify with the thrust and logic of the laws. Laws and culture are consistent. When this is not the case, laws are only as effective as the power of their enforcement. In the same way, institutions such as schools reflect a society's usual ways of thinking about them, as do markets, churches, and voluntary organizations. Therefore, to anticipate the effectiveness and stability of public institutions, we have to take into account the institution's clients and the degree to which the clients' culture and sense of belonging match and support institutional forms and practices. But we tend to take this reciprocal relationship for granted and even try to export institutional forms from one society, where culture supports them, to another where it will not.

The very legitimacy of government depends on this identifying process. For example, consider the Philippine government's problems over the years in dealing with its Muslim minority. When central government institutions such as the National Police or Constabulary, the justice system, or the school system have been extended to serve the Moro population in Mindanao, the Moro response has been less accepting than desired. These are the institutions of a large and distant national society to which Moros—from their point of view—have not belonged. The diagnostic problem, then, in seeking national-level institutional answers for ethnic conflict problems often is to determine whether the scope of a given institution's implied society matches the sense of meaningful *social universe* of the groups involved. Do ethnic clients see the institutions involved as "ours" and user-friendly, or as alien impositions?

Sociologists have long been interested in differences in the way institutions operate as a function of the size and complexity of the societies they serve. Folk and urban societies are typically contrasted, and sociologists, among other social analysts, have been concerned with the problems that come up when people who are programmed to think "folk" and are used to living with folk-sized institutions move to urban environments where the sheer size of society and complexity of institutions overwhelm them. They have trouble identifying with, and feeling themselves a part of, an impersonal mass society.

In effect, people develop a sense of their own meaningful social universe—that collection of people with whom they recognize identity and feel a sense of mutual obligation and duty. They think of themselves as connected to a ring of people who can be expected to be helpful and for whom one can expect to make sacrifices or undertake efforts for group benefit. There is a feeling that what is good for this "imagined community"—to use Benedict Anderson's descriptive terminology—is also good for the individual.[2] Therefore, in sorting out ethnic conflicts, it is useful to consider just what constitutes an effective social universe for the people involved, for solutions to conflict will have to make sense in this context.

---

[2] Benedict Anderson, *Imagined Communities: Reflections on the Origin and Spread of Nationalism* (New York: Verso, 1991).

An example of a relatively expanded sense of meaningful social universe is seen in the following exchange reported by a colleague who, when he was lecturing to an American military group, had been trying to emphasize the importance of calculating effective national loyalties. As I remember his account, he singled out an officer: "Captain, where are you from?" It turned out that he was from a modest town in the state of Oklahoma. Then he asked, "Captain, would you be willing to risk your life for the United States of America?" The answer, a resounding "Yes Sir!" But when asked whether he would be willing to risk his life for the state of Oklahoma, the answer was a confused confession that he had never considered the possibility. Then, how about your hometown? Answer: "No way!"

A number of years ago, a team of sociologists working on social change and development problems in African nations used the term "scale" to describe this phenomenon. In general, Africans had been living in very small psychological social universes. Sometimes the extended family was the outer limit and loyalties did not go much beyond that. Or it might have been a village or a clan. And in these cases, institutions matched a social environment in which people met face-to-face, communicated verbally, recognized relatively few specialized roles, and did not have to deal with strangers. Such a society is small in the scale of recognized human relationships. "Scale" seems an apt term and is useful here.[3]

When new countries are constructed by combining a collection of such separate social universes into one political entity, national-level institutions that assume a national sense of scale for effective operation will find that expectations may exceed the identifying capacity of

---

[3] Godfrey Wilson and Monica Wilson, *The Analysis of Social Change* (Cambridge: Cambridge University Press, 1945).

the clients. And, of course, in the short term, that is, within a few generations, these do not work. People are not inclined to pay taxes for the benefit of people they do not know; they will not place confidence in public servants who are strangers and play roles that are foreign to local culture; and they certainly do not think "civic society." They are not ready to cooperate with people who might not even speak their language, nor with officials whose behavior cannot be understood or predicted.

In an era of modern communication including radio and television, travel, and a pervading interdependent commercial world, the exact limits of scale in each case of ethnic conflict become blurred. It is apparent that, for many people, a sense of effective social universe changes with the subject. But note how this concept applies to ethnic conflict. For the *issues involved*, the outer limits of effective social universe have stopped at the corresponding level of ethnic identity. It does not mean that people cannot, or do not part of the time, think in terms of being part of a larger social universe to which they can extend loyalty or make sacrifices, but that for the issues in conflict, they have drawn the lines.

Therefore, when solutions that are proposed for resolving conflicts ask the contesting parties to think and identify with some larger ring of society and its well-being, what is being asked and what counts is a change in mindset regarding the social universe. In some cases, the mediator might in fact be able to elicit such a shift to another available mindset, as people may well identify variously from occasion to occasion with differing scales of society in their region. Usually, however, this is asking for too much too quickly, especially while memories of violent conflict are fresh. This can be seen in dramatic ways when refugees finally return to their ethnically mixed communities after a conflict is ended. The cases of Bosnia and Rwanda in 1996 stand out. The sense of tolerable social universe had diminished with the conflict. A former nonconfrontational inclusiveness had been shattered, and out-groups could not move back in.

Note that the limits of an actual shared culture, and of a felt social universe, may not coincide. Either can be more inclusive than the other. There are cultures, traditional and folk for example, that, while technically extending across broad geographical areas, reflect the way of life of small social universes. Somalia in the early 1990s seemed to present such a case: a common language, customs, pattern of values, religion, and so forth were shared over much of the area. But it was a culture that was consistent with village life, with institutions that operated at the local level. And it worked reasonably well when people conducted most of their lives at that level. However, when Somalian independence called for institutions that would operate at a national level—government, legal authority, commerce and economic activity—there was little in the traditional culture, with its local level of identities, to support institutions that were intended to operate on a national-scale conception of social universe. Thus when things came apart at the national level, the central government did not have enough moral or customary authority for resolving conflicts among contesting groups which saw themselves as separate societies unto themselves.

Conversely, many national societies do enjoy at least an overlay of national-level identity in their populations even when subcultures exist. Malaysia comes to mind, among many others. However, it is logical to expect that when groups maintain special interests as *ethnic* groups, and when language, customs, and ethos establish social boundaries within a larger population to the point of defining lines of conflict, easy acceptance of a recognized national-level social universe will be limited. The question is which scale of identity will take priority as solutions are proposed.

The scale concept, then, has practical significance for the way people perceive and respond to problem-solving initiatives. We will explore a few of these more central mindset considerations. In doing so, it is important to keep in mind that the outside mediator or practitioner will probably come into the conflict situation projecting the idea that the felt social universe *ought* to be much larger than that actually held by the parties to the conflict.

Where the Scale of Meaningful Social Universe Has Implications in Addressing Ethnic Conflicts

Mindsets Regarding Governmental Legitimacy and Authority

From an international perspective, we will most likely assume that national governments and their subdivisions should be in charge and expect that solutions to conflict should be sought within an existing national governmental framework. Members of an ethnic group concerned with their own problems are less likely to assume that legitimacy.

If what people think of as their social universe is confined to the ethnic group, then legitimacy, as culturally defined, will also be stuck at the ethnic level where authority is sanctioned by values, religious systems, and traditional patterns of leadership. Thus legitimacy at the national level, often having been formulated from an imported set of civic society assumptions, may be seen as an alien legitimacy, with authority being exercised by "them" rather than by "us." The result is that as solutions to conflicts are sought through compromise at the level of *national* government, discussion proceeds at cross-purposes if ethnic groups, national government officials, and outside mediators differ in their conceptions of the size of the social universe that is meaningful when remedies are considered. Rule by majority vote, for example, may have uncertain appeal.

Hence the dilemma for using the election process for establishing legitimacy. Political parties tend to form along ethnic lines. In power, they administer along ethnic lines, defend their ethnic ground, and see no virtue in any new electoral process to assure the will of all the people. Those who lose do not become the "loyal opposition." The Democratic Republic of the Congo (formerly Zaire) and Nigeria have been such cases, with the possibility that elections and party politics might have actually exacerbated ethnic conflict rather than diffused it; the occasion for conflict had become institutionalized. In Nigeria despite adoption of constitutions from time to time which have stipulated that political groups must not form along ethnic group or locality lines, no political culture existed that would make such an emulation of British political processes work. Not only were local regions dominated variously by Hausa, Fulani, Ibo, and Yoruba, the nation was segmented by religious gulfs with Islamic traditions prevailing in the north. This demonstrates that it takes more than codification of political culture in a constitution to make people really feel that "national" well-being is synonymous with local ethnic group well-being. The result in Nigeria has been near disintegration of the state.[4]

Administering Justice

Justice can come to mean many different things from the perspectives of differing cultures. Consequently, ad-

---

[4] For a collection of articles on this subject including items on Nigeria and Zaire (now the Democratic Republic of the Congo), see Harvey Glickman, ed., *Ethnic Conflict and Democratization in Africa* (Atlanta, GA: African Studies Association Press, 1995).

ministering it and accepting it can be a matter of some confusion. In part this is a function of differing values and norms, as we noted above, but in part it is also due to differences in assumptions about the scale of society in which one's sense of justice is anchored. Justice as seen from a civic society formulation and the perspective of a larger body politic is not likely to mean the same thing as when defined within a narrower ethos or from the experience of an ethnic group. Receiving "equal justice under law" may not be a happy prospect when the "law" and the concept of "justice" that goes with it derive from moral outlooks that are basically alien or, like a second language, have to be learned as a second way of thinking outside the context of one's own group and mores. Even in established Western democracies, there is a degree of difference in political philosophy regarding justice as reflected in British Common Law and the Napoleonic Codes of France. In ethnic conflicts, the differences which come up in the political cultures and philosophies that define justice are much greater.

The end result is that outside mediators may find that their search for just solutions that appeal to all will be less enthusiastically embraced by ethnic groups than expected. Justice becomes a relative matter, and especially relative to the sense of scale of society to which it is to apply. The conception of justice that serves the needs of a multiethnic society, for example, may not feel like justice to the separate groups that make up that society.

Appealing to Respect for Human Rights

The international community's concern for human rights and for applying humanitarian standards in its intervention often seems to be greater than that exhibited by the parties actually in conflict. One question is who qualifies as "human." As in international warfare and conflict in general, moral restraint seems to lose relevance as foes are seen as something less than human and less deserving of the group's usual standards of treatment. Sometimes attempts to administer humanitarian relief can be impeded for the same reason. Relief administrators are often frustrated by a lack of the kind of cooperation that they would expect from actions based on evenhanded policies and a sense that everyone in the larger community deserves attention according to need. Even in expediting distribution of basic food or medicine, the designation "human" becomes highly relative. When governments that are presumed to be in charge of an area bend relief efforts to their own narrow political or ethnic group advantage, or allow theft and corruption in handling relief goods intended for people beyond their sense of social responsibility, problems are compounded. Having to bribe one's way to get relief goods through customs or hire one's own security guards as protection against a supposedly friendly population is a severe blow to the altruistic outsider's values.

This clash of mindsets again goes back to a definition of just how large a circle qualifies for sympathetic consideration: perhaps the ethnic group, perhaps the village, perhaps only the family. Thus when conflict managers expect to take the moral high ground for carrying out human rights and humanitarian efforts in accord with civic society assumptions that everyone is "human," a basic and painful clash in outlooks can be expected. Rwanda was a case in point. Over the years, Hutus and Tutsis had apparently adapted to what hopeful development administrators believed to be an evolution toward a civic conception of society. But the eruption of wide-scale barbarity in the massacres of 1995 indicated that the levels of psychological identity and the sense of just who is human had been little enlarged.

How Public Officials Define Public Service

The details of managing ethnic confrontation are usually the responsibility of local public officials. The key word is "public." What does it mean? What collection of people makes up a recognized "public"? Where ethnic identities are strong, especially in new nations where the idea of civic society is more theoretical than real, public officials may hold a rather narrow conception of the "public interest" (some languages lack even the words for expressing the concept). Consequently, the expectations outsiders have of officials and leaders being motivated by a more comprehensive sense of the public interest may be unwarranted. The result is outrage when the outsider learns that to a local official, "public" means only that official's ethnic community or an even smaller social universe. The outrage is the greater when graft and corruption appear to be sanctioned accordingly.

Often the problem is that *formal structures* of governmental institutions have been transplanted rather artificially into newly formed national societies where no psychological sense of social contract encompassing the whole society had existed. Officials are caught in this dilemma along with their constituents. Their felt responsibility goes first to what they perceive to be their own people, so that partisanship can easily run along family, clan, or ethnic group lines rather than national ones. Again there is a mismatch in expectations as to a leader's role within the ethnic group on the one hand and within a nation-state on the other.

Perhaps it is more accurate to say that officials and leaders in these cases often are people with multiple identities. In one part of their minds they do think in terms of their total national societies and, at least intellectually, are able to think of a broad public interest. But when there is no corresponding expectation from the constituents that matter most to them, the responsibility dilemma persists.

The Problem When Sense of Identity Seems to Expand or Contract Depending on the Issue

Along with the officials mentioned above, ordinary people can also hold a flexible sense of who they're connected with and can therefore switch from one scale of identity to another as the context and issues change. For instance, a person might grow up with a well-defined ethnic identity, but attend a multiethnic school that competes in soccer with other schools, learn a second language, work in a factory with a multinational trade name, join the national army, enter a profession, or get rich—all sources of identity which might cut across the original. The challenge in proposing solutions to conflicts is anticipating when and in connection with what subject a deeply held *ethnic* definition of social universe will take precedence in a segment of a population that is otherwise accustomed to thinking in terms of a national or possibly larger identity. The objective usually is to pose solutions to problems in a way that will avoid pushing the ethnic button all over again.

In predicting reactions to steps aimed at easing confrontations it is also useful to recognize that in most societies people routinely live in both primary and secondary circles of meaningful social relationships. Ethnic identity and the outlooks that go with it will be strongest at the primary level where people meet face-to-face and know each other by name. The difficulty is that the outside mediator will probably focus first on the kinds of solutions that, from a local *ethnic group's point of view*, pertain more to its secondary identities: policies of the national government, economic institutions, law and order, a range of civic organizations. This is obviously advantageous if people are able to accept them on the basis of their larger sense of identity. But when aspects of proposed solutions cross the line into those matters that relate to a group's primary sense of significant social relations, perceptions and judgments are processed accordingly, that is, in ethnic terms.

Further, the outlooks that are most important when the chips are down will tend to be those that are most laden with value and emotion, and thus those most associated with a sense of social universe that ends at the boundaries of the ethnic group. Feelings of morality and of how things ought to be, of security in social interaction, pleasure and displeasure, sentiment, personal worth and dignity, and duty and responsibility develop at the primary level. The significance of primary associations will differ enormously from place to place, of course. Where some people will live their lives with people much like themselves in school, their residential area, and the workplace, others will grow up in a mobile environment and expect to conduct more of their meaningful activities in a range of more impersonal secondary relationships.

Consequently, when issues can be recast so that they are perceived to relate to a secondary scale of society, in effect defusing the primary worldview, an advantage in problem solving might be gained. Sometimes having a common enemy recognized by all local groups serves the purpose, as will common goals. But simply preaching against narrow views of what constitutes the social good predictably will not be very effective, although that common good might be understood intellectually. And attempts to educate toward a more civic view of the local social universe will proceed much more slowly than optimists expect.

It might be pointed out, parenthetically, that this also applies to attempts at empathy-building in conflict resolution efforts that use intergroup experiences, workshops, or other educational processes to help people gain a sense of common humanity with the other group or with the national society. The idea is that in living and working together, participants will come to know their opposites and discover that they can get along with them. But however successful such brief exercises staged at a secondary range of association might be, primary identities and loyalties will still count most. This helps explain the disappointment that facilitators have reported in the course of discussing projects in Israel, for example, when groups of Israelis and Palestinians have become good and apparently empathizing friends in the course of a several-week intergroup activity only to admit with deep emotion at the end that should the occasion arise, they would still have to consider the other an enemy and treat that person as such.

Meaningful Social Universe Is a Function of Geography and Demography

When the geographical space that people live in and their ethnic boundaries coincide, the outer limits of felt solidarity as an ethnic society are logically reinforced, depending, of course, on the ease and degree of communication and interaction that prevail throughout the area. When one government equals one ethnic group, institutions tend to function smoothly because they enjoy uniform cultural sanction whether the society is considered authoritarian or democratic. Or when a desire for political independence follows the lines of cultural homogeneity, this becomes self-determination, with the "self" part already defined.

The difficulty comes, as we know all too well, when more than one ethnic group, each with its own culture and sense of social universe, occupies the same geographical space without an overall accepted expectation that the conventions of civic society will apply.

This is evident especially in the nationality problems left over from converting colonial administrative boundaries into the boundaries of independent nation-states.

The geographic logic that suited the convenience of colonial administration did not necessarily match the geographic logic of the local population's shared social universe; in many cases the boundaries cut across the lines of ethnic groups. While colonial powers may have tried to encourage the idea of carrying on in a spirit of civic culture, and while some new governments may have been able to manage diversity in varying degrees, a much closer coincidence of geography and an integrating sense of national identity would make it much easier for governments to carry out their essential function. The prospect is that either the geographic boundaries will have to change or the sense of effective social universe will have to expand.

This sets the dilemma for managing contemporary conflict: Can one expect political culture to change and ethnic identity to expand fast enough to defuse ethnic conflict? It would appear that the international community has been unrealistically optimistic. In any case, when demography is unrelenting, the task is greatly compounded.

5

Fifth Problem Area: Legitimizing the International Community's Role in Addressing Ethnic Conflict

A final area in which we see mindsets playing a significant part is in the *ways of thinking by which the international community and its representatives feel called upon to intervene* in managing ethnic conflicts in the first place, and in turn, the *ways of thinking by which ethnic groups react to such intervention.*

There is a point in posing the standard question that is routinely asked in analyzing administrative behavior: What is the expected function of the institution in question, and what are the proper role expectations for the people involved? The difference here is that the context is a global society. The question then becomes what—when ethnic conflict gets out of control—do people really expect the United Nations or its agencies to do, or expect regional blocs, peacekeeping forces, major countries acting on their own initiative, or the many NGOs that have occasion to be involved to do? In short, what role or roles are international institutions and their personnel expected to play? These role expectations will have both a formal side—as spelled out in such things as United Nations resolutions or treaty agreements—and an informal side, as carried in the mindsets of everyone concerned. At the field level, this informal side becomes important first in the way that outsiders expect to conduct their activities and, in turn, in the kind of cooperation received by those who view the operations from the inside. Informal expectations also play a significant role in establishing recognized *authority* for carrying out conflict management operations in the first place, both as authority assumed and as authority accepted.

All this is closely related to the discussion in the previous section concerning the sensed scale of meaningful social universe, for in the course of having to address a rash of ethnic conflicts in the international relations system, two trends seem to be going in opposite directions. On the one hand, in an ever more intensely interacting world society, where economic and political institutions operate on a global scale, increasing numbers of people have come to think in terms of being part of a very large social universe and to think of international institutions as normally acceptable parts of international life. Yet, as noted earlier, for other people—indeed, the vast majority worldwide—the largest sense of social universe with which they can seriously identify remains, at best, variously the clan, tribe, local ethnic group, or nation.

Therefore, practitioners trying to manage ethnic conflict constantly face the difficulty that expected role behavior is ill-defined for doing what has to be done. And it is ill-defined as seen from both sides of the intervention. Who has the responsibility to do something when violence escalates? By what right is intervention engaged in? Or, conversely, to what extent do ethnic groups in difficulty have the right to *expect* outside intervention as part of the solution to these problems? And what, as a matter of expected role behavior, are the intervenors sanctioned to do?

We need to recognize that in this modern era, more people, including members of ethnic groups in conflict, can, in fact, think in terms of being part of an international community—at least part of the time. The question is how much and in what circumstances? I recall occasions during the time I was serving abroad when American election campaigns were in full swing back home. Sometimes local people would comment that they wished that they too could vote in American elections, because they thought it would mean more for their lives than votes in their own country! That is a real awareness of international interconnectedness.

Degree of expanded outlook is important because when problems come up, the way that members of an ethnic group orient themselves in terms of an international community has much to do with their perspective both on issues and on their own sense of the societal context within which issues can be resolved. Perhaps even more important, it has much to do with the degree of legitimacy accorded to the international institutions and the international personnel that try to address and resolve conflicts. It is interesting to note that in many cases outside authority is more acceptable than locally contested authority. American soldiers patrolling Haitian communities enjoyed a certain popular acceptance; even minimally armed UN forces from very small nations are accorded respect as representatives of some kind of world-level authority. To refugees in Gaza, for example, they represented something of a lifeline.

A sense of supranational identity is already apparent in the motivations of international practitioners themselves as they work with distant conflicts. Humanitarian services start with a concern for the well-being of all people. For those carrying out the activities of the long list of NGOs heavily involved, a world-scale sense of responsibility lies at the very foundation of the philosophy by which they work. Many conflict managers are already international civil servants, and those representing single governments reflect a broad conception of national interests in an interdependent world. These efforts are supported by an increasingly internationalized public constituency. Especially since the end of the Cold War, collective effort on the part of the international community is generally seen as the best way to address ethnic conflict problems. The stature, or at least the potential stature, of the United Nations as the leader and coordinator has been tenuously augmented accordingly. An international role in managing ethnic conflicts is gaining experience and precedent.

Putting all this together, we can expect that on the receiving end of international intervention, ethnic groups will also become increasingly aware of their belonging to an international community in the way that they look at their own problems and in their readiness to involve the international community in resolving them. At least leaders will, and many of their constituents may also, depending on their degree of isolation or involvement with the wider world. As a bit of unfortunate evidence of this awareness, terrorism itself is based on a very real consciousness of international forces and the possibility of manipulating them. The prospect of gaining outside attention through terrorism may well be seen as the resource of choice in an otherwise bleak set of local options for advancing a cause or expressing grievances.

We are thus led into considering several interesting points in political philosophy and speculating on what the future holds for our collective ability to manage ethnic conflicts. Basically the question is if people, both at the ethnic-community level and at the nation-state level, begin to expand their sense of meaningful social universe, will they come to take it for granted that supranational institutions will and *should* serve the special needs of a global community? Will some form of an *international* civic culture emerge to support and give legitimacy to international efforts when ethnic conflicts erupt?

Since the end of the Cold War, we have begun to turn more to international agencies as the proper avenue for doing something about ethnic conflicts that concern the international community, including those that take place entirely within the boundaries of sovereign nations. The difficulty is that international organizations lack a true international constituency—a critical mass of people across national boundaries that really expects these agencies to function as institutions of a global society. In sociological terms, they are not yet fully institutionalized in the thought patterns of a world citizenry. Agencies such as the United Nations have developed faster as ideal formal structures than they have as a set of organizations generating the reciprocal popular expectations that would sustain their functions as normal procedure. Again the case of Bosnia stands out. The question of whose responsibility it was, and what the citizens of the countries that might do something about it would support, delayed action for a critically long time. And for the decision makers at that time, estimating the risks involved included making judgments as to the way that parties to the conflict would perceive the legitimacy of outside intervention—and react to it. It was hard enough to calculate the military situation in the area and the logistical demands of intervention. Calculating the psychological probabilities behind it all was much more difficult.

At the present time, international organizations hold formal authority only by the votes and cooperation of their nation-state members; their operating procedures and sense of purpose have to reflect the formal political processes by which sovereign member states conduct their international affairs. Hence, international organizations find themselves in an awkward stage in the process of maturing. In effect they are looking for psychological support in the minds of a maturing international body politic, or more progress in a transition toward the kind of international civic culture mentioned above. This would sustain in a new way the credibility and viability of, for example, the United Nations itself, regional organizations, peacekeeping forces, human rights groups, and NGOs engaged in relief activities. If international institutions exist only as agreements on paper, or as delegated entities subject to the pleasure and votes of rigidly sovereign states, they have a limited legitimacy for taking action when ethnic confrontation begins to go out of control.

Thus, as public expectations change, we may be witnessing a shift in the international public mindset relative to managing ethnic conflict. Rather than erratically calling on international organizations to take action as an extension of international politics or in pursuit of concerns defined at nation-state levels, remedies would be sought which reflected the world community taking responsibility *in the context of its conception of itself as a world community*. In effect, international organizations would be exercising their civic duty to address ethnic conflicts just as they would assume their duty to resolve other matters that pertain to an ever more interconnected and interdependent world.

Yet to make it really work, we reiterate that some critical mass of world citizens must identify, at least in one part of their minds, with an international community and support its activities as an extension of their own identities.

Actually, this is occurring at an accelerating rate. Note

some of the evidence of precedent-breaking developments. Global interdependence has prompted ever closer interaction of people in a vast array of activities and professions, so that the sheer number of people whose scale of social universe is already global has increased almost exponentially. Global corporations have become commonplace. A European common identity is slowly evolving, with commitment still hesitant, but enjoying nevertheless enough of a constituency that Europeans are doing things *as Europeans*.[1] And the sheer number of nongovernmental agencies that have become psychologically accepted internationally is adding to a critical mass of international identity.

Though in the United States it is still advantageous to assure the electorate that the United States will not give up its sovereignty by placing U.S. forces under foreign command, there is nevertheless a distinct preference for meeting ethnic conflict problems in a multilateral framework.

As this collective sense of social universe expands, those who manage ethnic conflict on behalf of international institutions will enjoy increased legitimacy and, with that, the normal expectation on the part of ethnic groups that outside help is both acceptable and desirable. This could come to be a very considerable factor in addressing future ethnic confrontations.

---

[1] There is an interesting discussion of changing identities, especially those of a younger German generation, in Marc Fisher, *After the Wall: Germany, the Germans and the Burdens of History* (New York: Simon & Schuster, 1995).

A Note on Analytical and Case Study Priorities

Having said all this, what are the implications for getting down to specific cases? When one accepts that mindsets constitute a basic reality to be dealt with in managing ethnic conflict problems and that they are largely rooted in ethnic culture, where does one start in undertaking an analysis or in ordering one's observations in field situations? What are we trying to understand with a culture and mindsets approach that we are not already trying to understand by other, more familiar means?

The quest for psychocultural understanding is an open-ended process, and conclusions are hard to prove. Details are limitless, and, in the end, one will probably have to live with the feeling that one's best analysis is only partly done. Thus the question posed for a brief summary here is what priorities are recommended as one starts analyzing a specific case of ethnic conflict.

Possibly the first question is how seriously one wants to try to pursue a psychocultural dimension. There is a tendency among international practitioners to consider such an emphasis "soft," as not practical or realistic. There is something of a mindset against it—to use our own terminology here. Real professionals supposedly focus first on the "hard" and more tangible aspects of statecraft and national interests. People who worry about culture appear to be impractical and idealistic, and psychologists seem to live in another world. Therefore, to devote analytical attention to mindsets is to be persuaded that they are, in fact, highly significant operative variables in ethnic conflicts, and that trying to address them forthrightly and objectively is a more productive route for achieving accurate understanding than simply depending on intuition and a set of implicit assumptions about human nature that have been learned out-of-awareness in some other place.

In trying to apply the discussion developed in preceding chapters to real conflict situations, we suggest an initial checklist of key concerns that typically come up in the process of managing ethnic conflict which, in turn, call for making culture and mindsets judgments. The reader may, and we hope will, think of others. While the list is far from exhaustive, it may help by establishing a logic for choosing priorities in an analytical quest that could, in a full-blown research project, go on for a longer time than the immediate conflict itself. The logic of working from operational priorities is important in itself in that it goes against a usual assumption that to achieve a cultural perspective, a whole culture has to be understood first. Such is an ideal approach, of course, especially in that having a whole system in mind helps to establish more accurately the meaning of the items within the system. But for the practitioner, there is much to be said for the ability to turn the procedure around and first analyze the activity being undertaken for those essential elements, such as pivotal implicit assumptions, that probably will be subject to culture and mindset differences. In negotiation, for example, mindsets regarding trust would be critically pertinent, and this would vary by culture. With this kind of acquired cultural sensitivity, the professional practitioner is better able to establish order in the inquiry—ask the right cross-culturally strategic questions—and then make the best use of the cultural information and advice that is available.

The twelve considerations for understanding ethnic conflict given priority here typically would be important in most ethnic conflict cases, either within the context of the conflict itself, or in relation to activities undertaken to manage it. They follow, of course, from the discussion presented in the preceding text.

1. How does the way that past events are perceived set the stage for confrontation? This is simply historical background, but history as carried in ethnic group culture, history as socially remembered. The task is to research the subjective history that people have learned at home, at school, or from their ethnic society. The analytical objective is to capture history as it has been culturally transmitted to establish where, psychologically, an ethnic group is coming from in its conflict behavior.

2. How do issues and problems in contention play on and trigger the sense of ethnic identity? Why is this the definitive factor in the way that people take sides? While the fact that conflict has arisen might make it seem that ethnic identity is the all-pervading factor, the details of the connection between issues and identity are important in attempting conflict resolution and prescribing remedies, because variation in the degree of attachment to identity can be critical.

3. What outlooks and positions on issues exist that simply will not be subject to negotiation? In a culture and mindset approach, there is no way to sidestep

the search for those ways of thinking that fall into the category of deep culture, are most emotionally loaded, are most institutionally reinforced as in religion, and are most likely to result in intransigence throughout a conflict. This direction of inquiry is fundamental to conflict management strategy.

4. What do people actually want and expect from government? The role of government, after all, is central to everything that is done to manage conflict or to repair the damages done by it. Pursuing this question is essential because what the outside intervenor assumes to be the proper function of government usually will not match the assumptions of ethnic groups involved. Patterns of thinking regarding citizen participation, accorded legitimacy, justice, law and order, and so forth are all subject to cross-cultural variation, as was discussed earlier.

5. What is the prevailing culture of public service and public administration? This follows from the last item and is an essential consideration for practitioners who have to understand the environment in which they are working. And mindsets in this regard differ notoriously across ethnic groups.

6. How have people come to think about their economy? Because economic matters are so often in contention in ethnic conflict and an economic strategy is so often a part of the conflict management process, a cross-cultural look at mindsets regarding economic circumstances, performance, real aspirations, and the way that economic institutions are to be organized is usually revealing.

7. In cross-cultural perspective, how are leaders and leadership defined? In ethnic conflict situations, the importance of leadership role behavior can hardly be overestimated, nor can the cross-cultural task in

understanding it. From the personal qualities expected in a leader to the privileges that go with position, culture and mindset analysis is essential, and this applies to leadership roles from the neighborhood level to the national arena.

8. How is conflict itself perceived? And what are the accepted prescriptions for handling it? Conflict, of course, is the central subject here, so differences in the way ethnic groups are programmed to avoid it, engage in it, or resolve it are items deserving close attention. There are ethical systems that apply to conflict behavior, and they are not universal; exacting revenge or willingness to be a martyr, for example, are valued differently from society to society. And compromise and forgiveness seem to be acquired tastes, differing by cultural prescription.

9. What differing perspectives and styles are brought into the negotiation and bargaining process? If these differ across cultures in the world of business and commerce, they can surely be expected to differ as ethnic groups negotiate in the course of conflict management. While world-wise leaders may be able to adapt to international negotiation styles, their constituents, in their perceptions of what has transpired, may not. This has important consequences in the way that agreements are accepted and carried out.

10. What reactions can be expected to using force and coercion, especially that used by outside peacekeepers? As choosing peacekeepers and supervising their activities are frequently a part of conflict management, perceptions in this regard can be critical. And because of the wide range of factors that come together to affect these outlooks, the analytical task is demanding and complex, and it is worth pursuing analytical projects and case studies on this subject alone.

11. Is there a cultural dimension to the way that humanitarian activity is perceived? Because this question addresses emotions and needs that would seem to be universal in nature, the possibility of important differences existing in the way that the outsider's most well-intentioned activities are perceived tends to be overlooked. But experience would place the question squarely on this checklist both for the key role that humanitarian activity plays in managing ethnic conflict and for the real contrasts in mindsets that affect it. From the meaning of life and death to outlooks on altruism, reciprocity, medical practice, or volunteerism, underlying patterns of thinking vary significantly.

12. How do psychocultural factors affect prospects for the economic and political development projects that often go with conflict management efforts? As development implies bringing in new practices and new institutions where they did not exist before, there is good reason to consider the culturally patterned ways of thinking that, on the one hand, may inhibit acceptance or, on the other, will be needed to sustain them. This is a rather large agenda item, one that needs to be broken down into its components for further examination depending on the particular project initiated. For example, inclinations to save money, motivation to work, or the outlooks that go with civic culture may be to the point in some aspect of development efforts. Still, by way of setting a priority agenda here, the subject comes up quickly.

To the above listing, an additional suggestion that applies across the board stands out for making culture and mindset explanations relevant. This is the need for analysts/observers, in making their judgments, to take into account social and cultural change, modernization, or trends toward international practices. This change process often makes up part of the conditions from which ethnic conflict arises. It is difficult enough to calculate probable mindsets at work when things are peaceful and culture is static. It is harder to analyze a moving target where psychocultural factors are in flux at both the group and the individual level. Still, when analyses and estimates can be calibrated for the changes that are taking place, the quality of understanding increases accordingly.

In any case, an important objective in undertaking a culture and mindset analytical approach is to reduce that portion of conflict behavior that appears irrational and unpredictable, and therefore unmanageable. Searching out the ways of thinking that seem most seriously "irrational and unpredictable" in the eye of the beholder as conflict resolution efforts are pursued will help add to the agenda sketched here. Managing the conflict might still turn out to be exceedingly difficult, but at least the damage due to misperception of conflict behavior and misattribution of motives can be reduced.

Bibliography

Anderson, Benedict. *Imagined Communities: Reflections on the Origin and Spread of Nationalism*. New York: Verso, 1991.

Avruch, Kevin, Peter W. Black, and Joseph A. Scimecca, eds. *Conflict Resolution: Cross-Cultural Perspectives*. New York: Greenwood Press, 1991.

Connor, Walker. *Ethnonationalism: The Quest for Understanding*. Princeton: Princeton University Press, 1994.

Druckman, Daniel. "Nationalism, Patriotism, and Group Loyalty: A Social Psychological Perspective." *Mershon International Studies Review* 38, Supplement no. 1 (April 1944): 43-68.

Fisher, Glen. *Mindsets: The Role of Culture and Perception in International Relations*, 2d ed. Yarmouth, ME: Intercultural Press, 1997.

Fisher, Marc. *After the Wall: Germany, the Germans and the Burdens of History*. New York: Simon & Schuster, 1995.

George, Alexander. *Presidential Decision-making in Foreign Policy: The Effective Use of Information and Advice.* Boulder, CO: Westview Press, 1980.

——. *Bridging the Gap: Theory and Practice in Foreign Policy.* Washington, DC: United States Institute of Peace Press, 1993.

Glickman, Harvey, ed. *Ethnic Conflict and Democratization in Africa.* Atlanta, GA: African Studies Association Press, 1995.

Gurr, Ted Robert. *Minorities at Risk: A Global View of Ethnopolitical Conflicts.* Washington, DC: United States Institute of Peace Press, 1993.

Horowitz, Donald L. *Ethnic Groups in Conflict.* Berkeley, CA: University of California Press, 1985.

Little, David. "Belief, Ethnicity, and Nationalism." *Nationalism and Ethnic Politics* 1, no. 2 (Summer 1995): 284-301.

——. *Sri Lanka: The Invention of Enmity.* Washington, DC: United States Institute of Peace Press, 1994.

McNamara, Robert S. *In Retrospect: The Tragedy and Lessons of Vietnam.* New York: Times Books, 1995.

Mojzes, Paul. *Yugoslavian Inferno: Ethnoreligious Warfare in the Balkans.* New York: Continuum, 1995.

Newsom, David. "Foreign Policy and Academia." In *Foreign Policy,* no. 101 (Winter, 95-96): 52-67.

Smith, Anthony. *National Identity.* Reno, NV: University of Nevada Press, 1993.

Steinberg, David Joel. *The Philippines: A Singular and a Plural Place,* 3d ed. Boulder, CO: Westview Press, 1994.

Vertzberger, Yaacov Y. I. *The World in Their Minds: Information Processing, Cognition, and Perception in Foreign Policy Decisionmaking.* Stanford, CA: Stanford University Press, 1990.

Wilson, Godfrey, and Monica Wilson. *The Analysis of Social Change*. Cambridge: Cambridge University Press, 1945.

Zimmerman, Warren. *Origins of a Catastrophe: Yugoslavia and Its Destroyers.* New York: Times Books, 1996.

Index